9 Traits
of a
Life-Giving
MARRIAGE

Sue Detweiler

Praise for *9 Traits of a Life-Giving Marriage*

"If you are married or looking to ever get married (again), then this is a must-read. This book is not just about how to have a great marriage; it's about how to change your expectations, embrace your differences, and love the other person for who they are today, faults and all. This is a real-life how-to book about everyday marriages, not idealistic marriages and big theories we wish we could live up to. This is a practical-use guide to making marriage work for you. Yes, it takes work! Read this book and grow your marriage."

RORY VADEN and AMANDA JOHNS VADEN, Author of *Take the Stairs* and Senior Partner at Southwestern Consulting

"As a life coach and author, we see many people who have created strategies for business success. But those same people frequently have no plan for success in the more important areas of the life they are living. In *9 Traits of a Life-Giving Marriage*, Sue shares clear and sensitive methods of interaction for being as intentional about success in your marriage as you would expect in business. We have been blessed with nearly fifty years of a marriage that has practiced these important principles. Without careful nurturing of the relationships, your business—or your marriage—will likely fail. Don't take that chance."

DAN and JOANNE MILLER, Authors, *48 Days to the Work You Love* and *Be Your Finest Art*

"Sue Detweiler is one of the most gifted and passionate Christian teachers I have ever known. Her obvious call and commitment to minister to needs of today's families is a breath of fresh air to any generation."

PASTOR BRAD MATHIAS, President of Bema Media/iShine and Author of *Road Trip to Redemption*

"Sue Detweiler is simply extraordinary! A gifted woman of God who serves with both grace and godly wisdom, she is a person of courage, integrity, transparency, and faithfulness to the call of the Lord in her life. She sees beyond what may seem to be the impossible and goes forward in Christ realizing that His promise makes all things possible! The Detweiler family has become a testimony of God's love in action. Their hearts exemplify the "Spirit of Adoption," as they seek to help the lonely and discouraged to understand their full acceptance and value in Christ. Having known Sue for more than fifteen years, I have developed a deep respect for her zeal for the Lord, her family, the lost, and the extended Body of Christ. The Lord has called Sue to great significance and purpose."

GLENN C. BURRIS, President, The Foursquare Church.

"The love of God is bursting out of Sue Detweiler—out of her home, out of her heart, and out of her mouth! This daughter of the King is definitely on the move for the Kingdom. And with a divine combination of wisdom, genuine grace, and an amazingly approachable spirit...she's getting us moving with her."

TEASI CANNON, Author of *My Big Bottom Blessing*

"How would you describe a *life-giving* marriage? Does that description define your marriage? A life-giving marriage doesn't just happen! It takes an intentional effort to develop the traits associated with pouring life into one another. In her powerful book, *9 Traits of a Life-Giving Marriage*, Sue Detweiler offers biblical wisdom and practical insights to strengthen and deepen marriage relationships. The stress of life has a way of pulling us apart, but this book builds connectedness, joy, and love for a lifetime."

KAROL LADD, Best-selling Author of *The Power of a Positive Wife*

"Sue Detweiler is one of the most perceptive women and gifted communicators I know. Her voice of encouragement and words of hope in *9 Traits of a Life-Giving Marriage* must be heard around the world."

PAM VREDEVELT, LPC, Bestselling Author

9 Traits
of a
Life-Giving
MARRIAGE

How to Build a Relationship that Lasts

SUE DETWEILER

Life Bridge Press

Published by Life Bridge Press
ISBN (TPB): 978-1-943613-00-7
ISBN (eBook): 978-1-943613-01-4

Cover Design by Genesis Kohler
Editing and Production by My Writers' Connection

Dedication

To my husband, Wayne:
You are the love of my life,
patient, gentle, and kind.
You walk in the fruit of the Spirit every day.
Your character and integrity provoke me to be a better person.
Our common love and loyalty for Jesus
have guided our lives and home.
Your encouragement strengthens me.
Your love surrounds me.
We are His workmanship,
and He designed us to be side by side,
sharing the good news of His message together.
What a joy!

Contents

A WORD FROM WAYNE

Being married is an adventure. Let's face it; we each bring habits and expectations into a marriage. None of us is perfect. I know I fall short as a husband; all men do. Just as every woman fails to be a perfect wife.

The words, "'Til death do us part," join us with a partner who has his or her own preconceived ideas of what a marriage is supposed to be like. Inevitably, we don't meet each other's expectations. We are each faced with the need to confront our own immaturity, weaknesses, and selfishness because marriage has a way of revealing what was previously hidden or suppressed.

When I dreamed of being married, I pictured myself as a man who would be strong, loving, affectionate, and kind. I was already a pastor. At the age of twenty-nine, I was used to having my own space and my own way of doing things. Suddenly, I was faced with being the leader in a home with a very strong woman who had ideas of her own. I also was charged with being a covering to a wife whose tenderness and vulnerability went far deeper than her confident exterior revealed.

God intends for each of our marriages to be masterpieces of His design. He transforms the broken pieces of our lives into a union with purpose and hope. That's what He did in our marriage. Over and over again, I have been amazed at how God has used our story to bring healing to other couples.

As Sue and I talked about the writing of this book, we debated whether we should co-write it. After Sue's book, *9 Traits of a Life-Giving Mom*, had so much success, we both agreed that Sue would write this book on marriage and I would be her coach, confidante, and support.

Having quite a collection of great marriage books, we realized that most of the books have been penned by the husband with the support of the wife. As such, this book offers a fresh perspective on the characteristics of a life-giving marriage. You'll notice that Sue's writing style may be more vulnerable and transparent than you are used to; she writes from the heart. And we both hope that what you read in the pages that follow will strengthen and encourage you in your desire to be a better husband or wife.

We do not feel called to present ourselves as experts. Our desire is to walk alongside you, honestly and transparently, in this journey of marriage. The One we look to as the main expert on marriage was never married, yet He speaks of the church being His imperfect bride. His name is Jesus Christ.

Are there things about Sue that I would like to change? Yes, of course. If I were writing this book, would I choose to describe the circumstances of our marriage differently? Yes, I would. A husband's perspective will always be different from that of his wife, just as every human being sees life from a unique vantage point.

Throughout my marriage to Sue, I have learned that the greatest thing I can do to be a better husband is to walk more closely and intimately with God. In relationship with God I find strength, wisdom, insight, boldness, courage, and power to lead my home with honor and integrity. It's a great exchange. I give Jesus my imperfectness, and He gives me His Holy Spirit as a guide, comforter, and encourager.

With confidence in the transformative power of God, I know He will use this book to encourage and empower you. God is the One who brings life, even out of death. In Him, we have the opportunity to diffuse all work of the enemy and embrace the creative work of God.

As you connect to God as your source and work to develop the traits explored within this book, I pray that the fruit of this communion will be a life-giving marriage.

Wayne Detweiler

Introduction

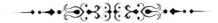

I still remember the moment I saw my husband, Wayne, for the first time. I was a lifeguard, wearing a sweatsuit with a whistle around my neck at a church camp in upper Michigan. He rolled into camp on a motorcycle, and I had to smile at his windblown hair and pink cheeks.

Wayne was the camp pastor for the week, in charge of spiritual enrichment for the junior high campers. We filled those seven days with long walks on the beach and hours of fireside talks about our life's dreams. In that short time, we developed a strong attraction for one another. I had never met a man who loved Jesus more than I did.

On the last night of our week together, we sat by the fire and Wayne said, "I sense we have kindred hearts. I want to stay in touch." My heart swelled as I agreed. I had already spent a night under the stars asking God to confirm what I was sensing.

At first, we wrote letters and cards and talked on the phone. We were able to spend more time together when he started seminary close to my college. Soon, we were ministering side by side as youth pastors at a church. As I grew closer to Wayne, I also grew closer to God. And the more time I spent with Wayne, the more I knew he was the one for me.

Do you remember the zing of attraction you felt when your relationship with your spouse was brand new? Being in the same room brought both comfort and butterflies. You felt empowered by the looks of admiration. Chills ran down your spine when your hands brushed together as you walked or reached for the popcorn.

Do you still have those feelings? Do you still get a rush when the love of your life walks into the room? Or has exhaustion, disappointment, or bitterness replaced the elation you once felt? With the starry eyes of new love, we all fantasize about how life could be together. We want to feel that same sense of excitement, joy, and fulfillment all the time. But that isn't reality.

If you have been married for more than a week, I'm certain you're aware that your marriage is not perfect. No marriage relationship is. And regardless of how wonderful or terrible your marriage may seem right now, I'm also certain that you are aware of ways it could be better, healthier, stronger, and more loving. We all desire to see positive changes in our relationships. We all want to be built up, encouraged, and empowered to live life to the fullest. Whether or not you use the exact words, what we want are *life-giving* marriages.

Unfortunately, so many marriage relationships limp along at less than life-giving; worse yet are the relationships that actively drain the life out of one or both partners. You may know someone in a hurting marriage; you may even be that person. And maybe, fearful of what others will think of your imperfect life, you're hiding that pain from your family and friends. You think to yourself, "Suck it up," or "Hang in there until the kids are grown," or "Nobody's marriage is perfect; this is just the way life is." You think, if you try harder, you can *just make it work*. Or, maybe you've reached the breaking point and are wishing for a way out.

The problem is that all wedded unions consist of *two* fallible, sinful, prideful, selfish human beings. But here's the good news: God is with you, too. With His help, you can improve your relationship with your spouse by being transformed into the person God created you to be. You are not alone in your desire to trade a boring or painful marriage into one that is full of joy, passion, and *love*; God wants all that and more for your relationship!

No matter the current state of your relationship, I am convinced that you can benefit from taking time to think, pray, and focus on your marriage. If your relationship is good, honing the nine traits of a life-giving marriage can make it even better. And if you're in a desperate place, uncertain if you can last one more night under the same roof as your spouse, please know that, with God, there is hope for a happier life *together*, when you develop the traits that reflect His likeness and character.

What are the nine traits of a life-giving marriage? Let me start by saying the following list isn't all-inclusive, rather, these traits provide a foundation for a strong, vibrant marriage. And after thirty-one years of being married to Wayne, I've learned that my commitment to living out these characteristics keeps my perspective pure and my priorities in place, and life is better. More importantly, our marriage is better. Here are the *9 Traits of a Life-Giving Marriage*:

Acceptance—Acknowledging the fact that God made you and your spouse differently empowers you to honor each other's unique roles and characteristics. Remember, despite your differences, you both bear the Creator's likeness.

Friendship—This is the bedrock upon which most relationships are built. Reinforcing this foundation can help you grow together, rather than apart, and keep your marriage stable and fun.

Safety—Emotional walls often feel like physical barriers that cut off feelings of happiness and security. Learn to recognize the warning signs and heal the wounds caused by an emotionally unsafe marriage.

Honesty—People who feel they can't express themselves honestly to their spouse often travel down a dangerous road to find someone who listens and understands. This chapter will help you set the ground rules that open the lines of communication between you and your mate.

Intimacy—A connection that includes, but goes far deeper than, sex, intimacy knits marriages together. To strengthen your bond, it's important to recognize and honor each other's differences and be intentional about meeting your spouse's needs.

Passion—It is possible to rekindle physical passion even if the fireworks in your relationship seem to have completely fizzled out. This chapter is a transparent discussion of one of our most basic and natural needs.

Endurance—The stress of life can push our emotions and our relationships to the breaking point. Well-placed faith fuels our endurance. But please know, this race isn't about survival; it's about experiencing God's best for your marriage.

Restoration—Understand this: Satan wants your divinely ordained marriage to fail. His battle tactics can cause injuries that, if left unattended, can certainly end in death. Restoration is a process of healing and building reinforcements to prevent future attacks.

Expectancy—Marriages typically begin with a healthy measure of hope and big expectations. Sin, in a variety of forms, can dash those hopes. Committing to a godly standard for your life and relationship will set you on a path to a strong, life-giving marriage.

Speaking of expectations, as we start this journey, I want to be clear about my intentions for this book. If you're looking for a quick fix to heal wounds caused by years of hurts and bad habits, you may be disappointed. This isn't like a fad diet meant to get your marriage in shape in six weeks or less. A good, strong, healthy, life-giving marriage will take work—for life. With that understanding, you'll discover that this book is for you if:

- You want to be honest about your struggles and overcome obstacles.
- You want to gain greater intimacy with Jesus and your spouse.
- You are willing to own your part and make changes in your approach to your relationship.
- You are willing to forgive your spouse for his or her part.
- You are willing to turn away from destructive patterns and cycles in your marriage.
- You want the light of God to shine through you, as you are transparent before Him.

I pray that the message in this book will help you to look up. Let it be a signpost to invite the Lover of your soul, Jesus, into the intimate issues of your heart and marriage.

Jesus was talking with His close companions when he said:

Remain in me, and I will remain in you.
For a branch cannot produce fruit if it is severed
from the vine, and you cannot be fruitful unless
you remain in me. Yes, I am the vine; you are the
branches. Those who remain in me, and I in them,
will produce much fruit. For apart from me
you can do nothing.
John 15:4-5 (NLT)

Being connected to Jesus is what gives us life. *He* is the Life-Giver. The life-giving joy, power, and purpose for marriage flow from the One who created us to be in relationship with each other. Apart from Him, we can't do anything.

As you journey through *9 Traits of a Life-Giving Marriage,* I hope you'll surrender freshly in your relationship with Jesus Christ. Allow the Holy Spirit to breathe new life into your marriage. Embrace the creative power of God to turn any mediocre (or miserable) place in your marriage into a masterpiece of His design for you as a couple.

Acceptance

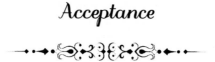

Embracing Your God-Given Gift
Affirming the Uniqueness of Who You Are
Welcoming the Difference of Your Spouse
Respecting the Rights of Their Ability to Choose
Choosing to Courageously Change Yourself
Trusting in the Transformative Power of God
Enduring the Tough Times
Believing God for Better Times to Come
Enjoying Each New Day in Every Season of Life

TRAIT 1
Acceptance

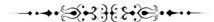

Face down, I cried out in desperation to God. My tears soaked the carpet as I poured out my heart. While my baby slept soundly in her crib, I pleaded for peace. In desperation, I begged for a resolution to the anger and frustration I felt toward my husband.

Our denomination had sent us to a Nashville suburb to plant a church seven years earlier. The weight of pastoring the church as a stressed-out young couple with a new baby had pushed me to the breaking point. We were pouring ourselves out to serve the needs of our flock, and in the process, we neglected the need to pour into each other. *Everything* about life felt hard.

God let me complain like a spoiled child, and I made sure to mention every one of my griefs, including all of my husband's faults. I knew *I was right*. God would surely see my husband's weaknesses and take my side. As I prayed aloud, all the private thoughts that had plagued my mind for weeks tumbled forth. In great detail, I told God how my husband should be acting:

"God, my husband is supposed to be the head of the house. He doesn't spend enough time in Your Word. He needs to be a better leader…" The list went on and I paired it with comparisons to the way I believed I measured up in the areas where my husband lacked.

Finally, exhausted, I quieted my spent heart and listened for God's wisdom. Still face down on the floor, I waited. I wondered how He would vindicate my tears. He knew my miserable marriage couldn't take much more. What would He tell me to do? I waited expectantly for His voice and His wisdom to speak to my heart.

Listening for God's Voice

God's voice differs from our own. However, when we so badly want our own way, it can be dangerously easy to mistake our thoughts and emotions for God's wisdom.

So how do you know the difference? How do you know if God is really speaking to your heart? The answer: God's voice is always consistent with His Word. One guiding Scripture on gaining *His wisdom* comes from James 3:18:

> *But the wisdom that comes from heaven is first of*
> *all pure; then peace-loving, considerate, submissive,*
> *full of mercy and good fruit, impartial and sincere.*
> (NIV)

Wisdom from God brings peace and assurance to your heart. To hear His voice, you must be willing to submit to Him and surrender to His leading. His voice will be confirmed by the good fruit produced by the Word. When you surrender to wisdom from above that is impartial and sincere, you are able to act with both humility and boldness.

God's voice is always consistent with His Word

His wisdom is so pure and full of mercy that, sometimes, it surprises us. That's how I felt when God spoke to my heart that day in 1993. In the quiet aftermath of my tears, I heard the gentleness of God's whisper deep in my heart.

2

"Open your eyes. I want to show you how I have made your husband. You expect him to be like you. I fashioned you while you were in your mother's womb to be a visionary leader. I fashioned Wayne differently..."

As I listened, I remembered how Wayne's great love for God and his gentleness had drawn me to him. Yet somehow, I had begun to discount this attribute and the way God had made Wayne.

We sometimes forget that "gentleness" is a fruit of the Spirit (Galatians 5:26). When David wrote Psalm 18, He praised God for His gentleness.

> *You have also given me the shield of Your salvation;*
> *Your right hand has held me up,*
> *Your **gentleness** has made me great.*
> *You enlarged my path under me,*
> *So my feet did not slip.*
> Psalm 18:35-36 (NKJV, emphasis added)

This Psalm was written and sung when David had victory over all opposing armies and was anointed as king over all of Israel. David was a man of war, yet he celebrated God's gentleness. The Hebrew word that is translated here as gentleness means "condescension." David is describing how God reached down to save his life and shielded him from the enemy. God gave David the physical and emotional strength he needed to survive. This gentleness reminds us of when Jesus stepped down to come to earth and humbled himself, dying for our sins. It is God's gentleness that makes us great.

Through the years, I have meditated on this Scripture which describes Wayne's leadership in our marriage. God knew what I needed. I needed a man full of the Holy Spirit who would lead me with godly gentleness. My husband has enlarged the path under me. He has held me up and kept me from slipping.

I understand now that God has always had my best interests in mind. But I didn't comprehend back then that Wayne's gentleness was exactly what I needed. With my face down on the ground after my complaint, I heard God say to me:

"You are trying to make Wayne into your own image. You want him to be like I made you to be. Let Me show a picture of My gentle leadership in your life. Sue, you are the one who needs to change. The way you glare at him when he doesn't measure up brings a coldness in your marriage that is not from Me. The way that you speak to him is not only disrespectful, it is wounding to his masculinity."

Then God brought to my mind a horrific situation that had recently been in the news. On June 23, 1993, a woman named Lorena Bobbitt, in an insane moment brought on by the stress of domestic violence, used a kitchen knife to cut off her husband's penis while he slept. As I write about this conversation with God, I still remember how God used the brutality of that event to get my attention. To be clear, Wayne's and my relationship has never been abusive, but God wanted me to see the part I had played in damaging our marriage.

"Sue, when you speak to your husband with harshness in your heart, your tongue is a sharp knife that emasculates your husband. You need to *stop* speaking to your husband in this way. When you speak to your husband privately and in public, you need to speak to him with respect.

"I have designed him to be a gentle and kind pastor. He is a world changer. I made him differently than you. I am pleased with how I made him."

I wept again, this time knowing that rather than trying to change my husband, God wanted me to focus on changing my own behavior. Gently chastised, I asked for the Holy Spirit to change my heart and help me recognize and honor Wayne's strengths.

Learn Acceptance

In those moments of desperation and repentance, God taught me the value of *acceptance*. This essential trait of a life-giving marriage allows us to love and honor our spouse's God-given nature. Every human being is woven together by God in a unique way. You can either magnify your spouse's weaknesses, thereby causing strife with your scrutiny, or you can accept who God made them to be.

Interestingly, it is often the very traits that initially drew you to your spouse that you may have to come to terms with after you are married. For instance, you may have a husband who is a strong-willed leader; he knows what he wants and when he wants it. You may have been impressed by his confident demeanor and decision-making ability when you were dating. Now, those same traits make him seem overly opinionated. Or maybe you're married to a wife who is very detailed-oriented. While you were dating, you appreciated her planning skills and innate ability to efficiently organize her home. Now, it seems like all she does is nag and nit-pick you to get all the details right.

Acceptance can be hard! Sometimes it can feel like acquiescence. You feel like you are "stuck with the other person." You reluctantly put up with them while the life drains out of your relationship. That doesn't seem very *life-giving*. But stay with me, because acceptance can bring about beautiful change.

Experience a Miracle-Change

Acceptance is a conscious choice to receive your spouse as God made him or her. As a wife, you have the power to magnify the God-crafted personality of your husband. As a husband, you can lift up your wife's God-given characteristics. When you do, you not only change the way you perceive your spouse, but, over time, you also change his or her perception of *you* and of yourselves as a couple.

In response to God's reprimand that day back in 1993, I made a choice to only speak words of respect, words that built up my husband. My decision sparked a miracle-cure in our relationship. No, his personality did not change. But when I looked at him with eyes

> *Acceptance is a conscious choice to receive your spouse as God made him or her.*

of admiration, rather than glaring with condemnation, my husband's confidence level grew. As a result, our relationship experienced a miraculous change.

You may be thinking, "You don't know my husband and how difficult he is!" You are right; I don't know your husband. But I know that you chose him. Something about who he is fits with who you are. Otherwise, you would have chosen someone else. Or, more accurately, God would have chosen someone else for you.

When Wayne and I conduct marriage seminars, it isn't unusual for at least one man in the audience to turn to his wife and say, "See, you need to treat me with respect! If you would treat me like your Prince Charming, then everything would be fine." If you're tempted to point the finger at your spouse and demand that he or she changes *first*...don't. Your mandate for superficial acquiescence will not bring breakthrough, but it's a sure path to bitterness.

What we all need is a faith-filled perspective change. Trust in God's transformative power to change *your* heart. Acceptance is not fairy dust that makes you fall in love with your spouse again; it is the goodness of God wooing you to trust Him.

Enjoy the Uniqueness of Your Marriage

It's important to embrace the way God has made your spouse. It is also helpful to accept how God has made you. Understand that the way you two work and live and love together may not be the same as any other couple's relationship. There are no cookie-cutter marriages.

For far too many years in ministry, I believed that, if God had just switched our gift-mix, life would be better. If Wayne had my gifts and I had his, we would fit into the traditional Christian perspective of marriage.

Joyce and David Meyer felt pressured to change who they were early in their marriage. The church they were attending made it clear that Dave should be the one who taught the Bible study they were leading from their home. The couple tried to conform; Dave taught while Joyce kept silent. It didn't work very well. God had not designed them to be like that.

Just as Priscilla's name frequently appears before Aquilla's in Scripture because Priscilla was the primary speaker, Joyce Meyer is a natural communicator and teacher. Their gifts didn't need to be swapped. Neither did Wayne's and mine. You don't need to be or do something other than that for which God created you. God doesn't make mistakes. He uses us individually, even as He uses us together.

If you are feeling pressured to fit into some type of mold, relax and enjoy who God has made your spouse to be. Enjoy and embrace the distinct way you are made and look for all the ways you suit each other.

Opposites Attract

My parents personified the notion that "opposites attract." Dad was a hard-working visionary, who pioneered six corporations before he died. In the small town of Auburn, Indiana, he was a well-known leader. He loved everything big—big dreams, big parties, and big adventures.

Of course, he married someone very different from him. As a girl, my mom blushed and hid when anyone pulled out a camera. Even as an adult, she never wanted to be the center of attention. She was perfectly content to stay at home. She enjoyed private intimate parties, but Dad's success meant she often ended up hosting big celebrations.

The differences that attracted them to each other ended up causing great conflict. When I was a teenager, things came to a head. I grew so tired of the fighting and arguments that I wished they would get a divorce. I hated feeling the tension in our home. I

Author's Note: Acceptance does not mean that you should allow someone to beat you, rape you, control you, or violate your personhood. It also does not mean you should allow your spouse to maintain extramarital affairs or yield to sexual addiction. You may feel like all your choices have been stolen from you. The truth is that you can make the choice to get help. If you are in physical or emotional danger or your marriage has experienced the trauma of an affair, please use the resources listed in the back of this book and reach out for help.

also hated being caught in the middle of their rocky relationship. It was especially hard to hear my father tell me I was just like him and then have my mom share with me her frustrations about Dad's personality.

Coming to Peace

My parents finally came to peace in their relationship when I was out of the house. Dad had two brothers and a sister that went through divorce, and my parents saw the devastation it caused the children.

They made a decision to not divorce. At the time, it was not because they were head-over-heels in love with each other. Rather, they loved God and their family. So instead of each one constantly trying to "fix" the other, they put their trust in the transformative power of God. They realized, *finally*, that there is no such thing as a perfect husband or wife. God hadn't called them to change each other. He had called them to change themselves through His power. When they surrendered to that calling, they found a peace they never could have dreamed possible, while in the midst of all those arguments.

I share their story because I know at least one person who picks up this book will be ready to quit—to give up and walk away from his or her spouse. If that's you, I hope you'll reconsider. I don't know your situation. I don't know how terrible it is right

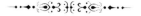

God can renew your marriage and transform it into something better than you can imagine.

now. What I do know is that God can renew your marriage and transform it into something better than you can imagine.

The Legacy of Your Choice

Even though I was an adult when my parents took a stand to not divorce, I am so grateful for their choice. Their decision marked the beginning of a turnaround in their relationship. They stopped trying to change each other. They accepted each other. Gradually they began to enjoy each other.

My mom, who has been widowed for many years, looks back at this time with a spiritual perspective. She sees the enemy's attack on her marriage. When they closed the door to divorce, they closed the door to the enemy. As long as the door was cracked, it let in hell's fury.

Now she sees Dad as the love of her life. The memories of their forty years of marriage—even the hard years—are a source of joy and an example to everyone who witnessed their transformation.

For Better or Worse

Many couples recite a version of these traditional vows on their wedding day:

I take you to be my (wife/husband),
to have and to hold from this day forward,
for better or for worse, for richer, for poorer,
in sickness and in health, to love and to cherish;
from this day forward until death do us part.

Every life-giving marriage embraces the changing seasons within a marriage and life. Your vow required that you not anchor your hope on your present feelings, but on the power of God to strengthen you and change you into His likeness.

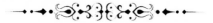

Life-Giving God,
I QUIETLY COME AND ASK YOU TO REFRESH ME
WITH THE RAIN OF YOUR HOLY SPIRIT.
RESTORE IN ME A CONFIDENCE IN YOUR ABILITY
TO TRANSFORM ME.
I CHOOSE TO CHANGE
MY DESTRUCTIVE THOUGHTS
INTO THOUGHTS OF HOPE.

I CONFESS THAT I AM NOT A PERFECT PERSON.
I HAVE SINNED AGAINST MY SPOUSE
IN WAYS TO WHICH I AM BLIND.
I AM NOT COMPLETELY AWARE OF THE WAYS
I HAVE SPOKEN DEATH INTO MY RELATIONSHIP.
I CHOOSE TO HUMBLE MYSELF.
I seek to see things like You see them.

FORGIVE ME, GOD, FOR THINKING THINGS THAT AGREE
WITH THE ENEMY OF MY SOUL.
JESUS, SHOW ME THE DOORS TO THE ENEMY
THAT I HAVE OPENED THROUGH UNFORGIVENESS,
BITTERNESS, AND A LACK OF FAITH.
FORGIVE ME FOR MY SELFISHNESS AND
SELF-CENTERED PERSPECTIVE ABOUT MY SPOUSE.
GIVE ME A PICTURE OF HOW YOU HAVE CREATED
_____ TO BE.
I OPEN MY HEART FOR YOU TO SPEAK TO ME
DURING THIS LIFE-GIVING JOURNEY.
I PUT MY HOPE IN YOU.
Breathe fresh life into my marriage.

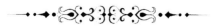

Friendship

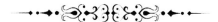

The Joy of Being Together
Sharing the Intimate Details of Your Life
Embracing the Pain and Sorrows of Another
Sharing the Joy, Delight and Triumph of Daily Life
Enjoying the Differences
Being Together in Oneness
A Powerful Bond
A Delicate Plant Needing Water and Nurturing
Thriving in the Sunlight of Love
Wilting in the Coldness of Contempt
A Daily Choice to Give Life or Death, Joy or Sorrow
Companionship or Abandonment

TRAIT 2
Friendship

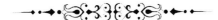

Not too long after we got engaged, Wayne came up with a plan for us to spend time with his brother's family. We were going to drive across the country to see his parents. I was excited! I actually looked forward to the twelve-hour excursion. Wayne and I had enjoyed a few road trips, so traveling with his brother, Dave, and sister-in-law, Martha, and their two young children, Dustin and Kyle, sounded fun. I imagined the four of us talking and laughing for hours, while the little ones played quietly and slept. Clearly, I had never before traveled long distances with children.

Dave and Martha arrived to pick us up in their Honda Civic. I was smitten by five-year-old Dustin, who immediately struck up a conversation with me. He looked so cute with his plaid shirt, crew cut, and lop-sided grin. I climbed in the back seat. Martha sat on one side, I sat on the other, and Dustin and eighteen-month-old Kyle were buckled in between us. We were off! *This was going to be so much fun*, I thought.

We'd driven only a few miles when Dustin asked, "Are we there yet?" It was the first out of roughly a million times that question popped out of his mouth. After a few hours, his endearing talkativeness had turned into irritating chatter, over which Martha and I tried to visit. Then Kyle began to cry. We didn't know it then, but the poor guy had an ear infection. He cried nonstop the rest of the trip.

Wayne's wonderful idea didn't feel so wonderful anymore. While Martha concentrated on comforting Kyle and I entertained Dustin, Wayne and Dave talked and laughed, completely oblivious to the frustration building behind them.

Of course, anytime we pulled over at a rest stop or to refuel the car and Wayne asked how things were going, I said, "Fine." I didn't want to complain or hurt anyone's feelings, so I bottled my own. But by the time we finally arrived at Wayne's family home, ice hung in the air between us. I was furious; my nerves were frazzled after spending hours in the car with a crying baby, and felt hurt because I'd been completely left out of the day's conversation. I had expected a fun day that would bring us all closer as friends. Instead of enjoying a road trip and bonding with my family-to-be, I'd felt trapped and forgotten in the back seat.

Forging a Forever Friendship

Though we were wildly in love, the rose-colored glasses came off before we got married. We fought throughout our engagement, not because we were at odds with each other, but because of the fears each of us was carrying down the aisle. Having seen my parents struggle in their relationship, I knew what I *didn't* want for my own marriage. So, in a naïve attempt to make our marriage perfect, I focused on both of our weaknesses and tried to *fix* our young relationship. I wanted to make sure we dealt with all our "stuff" before the big day. It didn't work very well.

As certain as I was that God had brought Wayne and me together, I prayed weekly (sometimes daily) that we would be able to work out our differences before we said "I do." Even from the early days of our relationship, it was clear to me that Wayne is a strong man. Certainly, he wants my best, but there are some areas—areas that I believed needed "fixing"—in which he was (and is) immovable. For that, I am thankful. Because, really, I wouldn't want to change my husband. Remember, he is who God made him to be. Not only that, but since I couldn't change him, I had to learn to trust God and realize that it isn't my role to act like the Holy Spirit in Wayne's life.

It wasn't until we got married that I embraced the fact that he was mine for life. What a relief! God had not only brought us together; He would keep us in His care. I relaxed into one of the most enjoyable times of our relationship, and life was good.

As newlyweds, we lived in a tiny trailer. I attended college, Wayne was in seminary, and we were poor and very happy. Wayne and I loved playing tennis at the nearby courts. (We would go from trailer to trailer knocking on the doors of our young married neighbors, until we found a couple willing to play doubles.) In our tennis shorts and shoes, we strengthened the bond of our friendship. In between studies, we played and enjoyed those honeymoon years. We went to the movies. We attended concerts. We hiked and went on picnics. And when bad weather cancelled our outdoor plans, we made love to the sound of the rain hitting the tin roof.

When Unity Unravels

Many relationships begin with positive, life-giving time spent together. What were some of your favorite things to do when you were first forming a relationship with your spouse? Do you remember how those activities and the time spent together drew you closer? You likely felt affirmed, appreciated, and encouraged. You enjoyed each other's company and spent time laughing while you got to know each other better. Your affection drew you together, and your passion seemed unquenchable.

So what happened? When did the honeymoon end? If you have been married for any length of time, you have had good

Time spent enjoying our relationships often gets relegated to an infrequent date night

days and bad days in your friendship with your spouse. Even in the strongest marriages, ups and downs can rock us to the core. Add in the stress brought on by common forces, such as work, children, debt, and extended family, and the time spent enjoying our relationships often gets relegated to an infrequent date night.

Marriage relationships often start in a whirlwind of romance and pleasure. The expectation is that those feelings of love and friendship will bloom and continue to grow. But in too many marriages, the opposite occurs. Instead of spending more time together, external factors take precedence. As life's demands pull at our attention and energy, we grow apart and those happy honeymoon days turn into a distant memory.

Friendship brings life to our marriages. And when friendship falters, the relationship is at risk of becoming a statistic. I'm sure you've heard that fifty percent of all marriages end in divorce. In *The Seven Marriage Principles*, John Gottman and Nan Silver explain the severity and consequence of this sad statistic.

> The chance of a first marriage ending in divorce over a forty-year period is sixty-seven percent. Half of all divorces will occur in the first seven years. Some studies find the divorce rate for second marriages is as much as ten percent higher than for first-timers. The chance of getting divorced remains so high that it makes sense for all married couples—including those who are currently satisfied with their relationship—to put extra effort into their marriages to keep them strong.
>
> One of the saddest reasons a marriage dies is that neither spouse recognizes its value, until it is too late. Only after the papers have been signed, the furniture divided, and separate apartments rented, do the ex-spouses realize how much they really gave up when they gave up on each other. Too often a good marriage is taken for granted, rather than given the nurturing and respect it deserves and desperately needs.[1]

---

[1] John M. Gottman, Ph.D. and Nan Silver. *The Seven Principals for Making Marriage Work*. New York: Three Rivers Press, 1999.

Maybe you are at a great place in your marriage and are experiencing the positive emotional connectedness of being one with your spouse. If so, great! What you learn in this chapter will help you strengthen your bond.

Alternatively, you may be secretly crying into your pillow, feeling as if your needs are unmet. You could be withdrawing to your workplace and flirting with the secretary who admires your leadership. You could be wondering if it's possible to regain the passion you once felt in your marriage.

Whatever the current state of your relationship, I know you picked up this book because you value your marriage. You want it to work. You don't want your marriage to end as a sad statistic. You want your marriage to be a rich, life-giving adventure. I want that for you, too! So let's continue in this life-giving journey together. I pray that God will reveal how you can revitalize your relationship and renew your friendship.

From Friends to Enemies

The fun days of playing tennis and going on long walks together came to an abrupt halt weeks after moving to Nashville. We had been married for a year and a half when our denomination sent us to Tennessee to plant a church from scratch. Our leaders laid their hands on us and sent us off with ample prayer and financial support.

We idealistically began our new adventure. We packed what few belongings we had and moved from our little trailer in Goshen, Indiana, to a suburb of Nashville. Trusting that God had called us, we had no idea of the life-threatening rapids we faced ahead. We saw the rainbow of God's promise and were blind to the Niagara Falls that the canoe of our marriage was about to tumble over.

Soon after arriving in Nashville, we signed up for a health club. My first afternoon at the club, I overdid my aerobics workout and injured my knee. Dragging myself home to our apartment, I fell again. This time, the torn ligament and cartilage around the knee couldn't support me.

Cell phones had yet to be invented. Rather than calling an ambulance, I waited for my husband to get home. I lay alone on the floor of my apartment, writhing in agonizing pain for several hours.

A few days later, I went to the hospital to have the ligament repaired. I'd never had major surgery before and a sense of aloneness overwhelmed me. I'm sure Wayne was with me, but I don't remember that. What I remember was that my feelings of loneliness were punctuated by the fact that all my relationships in the community were new; we were the pastors of a church that didn't exist yet. Aside from my husband, I had no other friends in the city. I had never felt so alone.

The first day home after the surgery, our relationship hit an all-time low. I was completely immobilized and in more pain than ever in my life. Since I couldn't go buy groceries, there was no food in the house. And, of course, since we didn't really know anyone yet; no church ladies stopped by with casseroles.

Before my accident, my husband joined a hiking club. He thought it would be a great way for him to meet people in our new town. Unfortunately, the first all-day hike took place the day after my surgery. After being in the hospital with me, he was probably ready to get outside. He left early in the morning for his ten-hour adventure without me. Hello, loneliness!

At home that day, my mind ran free with painful thoughts. *He was only thinking of himself. Doesn't he know I need him right now? How could he leave me and go off to hike with people he doesn't even know?*

In the middle of the day, excruciating pain set in; minutes dragged by as I watched the clock, waiting for Wayne to return. Aside from pain, I was starving. I tried to get up on my crutches, but it simply hurt too badly to move.

I had one phone number. I met our next door neighbor while on crutches in the hallway. (She had heard me screaming in pain a few nights before.) I didn't really know her, but I was desperate. I finally called her and asked if she could come over and help me get something to eat.

Afterwards, I lay in bed counting all the ways Wayne had wronged me that day. Little did he know that, when he opened the door after a wonderful day of hiking, he would face Godzilla. I had been wounded to the core of my personhood. I felt abandoned by him. Nothing he said held weight. Hateful words spewed from my mouth like fire.

I wish I would have known then what I know now. Our marriage was under attack by an enemy. Satan wanted to ruin our lives—our marriage—so we couldn't impact the community with the good news of God's redeeming love.

In addition to prayer and commitment, we had to learn to communicate. I know now we were making common marital mistakes. Whenever conflict arose between us, I became critical and contemptuous. Wayne defended himself by stonewalling and distancing himself emotionally and physically. Again and again, we struggled down this detrimental path. But once we learned to recognize the warning signs, we were able to choose a different road. You can, too.

The Apocalypse of the Four Horsemen

For more than thirty-five years, Dr. John Gottman and his team have studied marriages. As a research scientist, he uses rigorous methods and standards respected by medical science. The data he's gathered gives a scientific glimpse into the anatomy of a marriage.

In the family research laboratory, aka "the love lab," Gottman's team uses instruments to measure the heart rates of couples during conflict-filled conversation. They record the discussion and analyze the facial responses. During a ten-year study, with a ninety-one percent accuracy rate, they were able to predict which couples would divorce.

The couples whose marriages were not doing well often began disagreements with a harsh tone. Soon, the scientists watching would observe what Dr. John Gottman labeled as "The Four Horsemen." These four negative styles of behavior are lethal to a marriage and could lead to a chaotic end. Here is the list:[2]

HORSEMAN 1: Criticism. Criticism is more than a complaint. Criticism attacks character and blames the other person, "What is wrong with you?"

[2] Summary of principles from the book written by John M. Gottman, Ph.D. and Nan Silver. *The Seven Principles for Making Marriage Work,* 1999.

HORSEMAN 2: Contempt. Sarcasm and cynicism are common types of contempt. This disgusted attitude sometimes includes name-calling, mockery, sneering, or making jokes at the other's expense.

HORSEMAN 3: Defensiveness. Defensiveness denies responsibility and focuses all the blame on one's partner. "I'm not the problem; you are!"

HORSEMAN 4: Stonewalling. This is the last horseman to arrive, but the first one to parade off in silence. Stonewalling occurs when one partner shuts down or tunes out the discussion. They ignore the spouse with a coldness that is felt by everyone involved.

You may be thinking right now, "What should we do? The four horsemen not only know our names, but they regularly visit at our address." If you are experiencing criticism, contempt, defensiveness, or stonewalling in your marriage, you may be desperate for something to change.

A New Dance

A new beginning can occur right now, if you make a choice to change your behavior. If you have been stepping on one another's toes in this disappointing dance, shake up the steps. Decide today to relate to your spouse differently. You won't be able to control your spouse's words, tone, or behavior, but if you change *your* dance steps, you will change the dance.

Improving the way you relate to your spouse requires you to be purposeful about meeting his or her needs. Remember the acceptance we talked about earlier? These improvements won't come about by pointing your

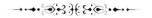

If you change your dance steps, you will change the dance.

finger and demanding that the other person change. You have to go first. In other words, lead by example.

Are you the best person you can be? Are you meeting your spouse's needs physically, intellectually, spiritually, and emotionally? Are you intimately connected at the heart, in spirit, in mind, and in body?

It's easy to fall into familiar behavior patterns. Automatic, blame-filled responses can keep you in a destructive cycle. But what if you change? *Really* change. To initiate true change in your marriage, challenge yourself to esteem the other person, to mend the relationship, and to commit to restore your friendship.

Esteem—Respect and value your spouse's uniqueness. Look with eyes of love. Speak with words that heal. Resist reacting and instead respond with love and patience. Change your dance step.

Mend—Repair the broken places. What has she been asking you to do that you just haven't made time for? What does he want that you haven't given him?

Restore—Don't look for immediate results. The reality is that your relationship could get worse before it gets better. Commit to your spouse and your marriage for the duration. Allow God's transformative power to restore your broken dreams and give you hope.

Rebuild Your Foundation of Friendship

Every healthy friendship needs to be nurtured. What did you do in building the friendship in your marriage? What were your favorite activities?

Make time for friendship. Go out and have fun. Leave the kids with a sitter. Focus on your marriage. Focus on building your friendship, rather than proving your point. If you do go out, make sure to lock up criticism, contempt, defensiveness, and stonewalling. They will ruin every date or party and eventually destroy every marriage.

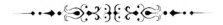

Jesus,
YOU ARE THE BEST FRIEND I COULD EVER HAVE.
YOU NEVER LEAVE ME OR FORSAKE ME.
YOU WROTE AN EVERLASTING LOVE LETTER,
FILLED WITH PROMISES FOR ETERNITY.

I CONFESS I HAVE NOT ALWAYS BEEN A BEST FRIEND.
I HAVE BEEN CRITICAL OF MY SPOUSE.
CONTEMPT HAS BEEN IN MY EYES AND ON MY LIPS.
I HAVE BEEN DEFENSIVE.
I THOUGHT THAT I WAS COMPLETELY RIGHT,
SO, I STONEWALLED AND GOT STUCK.

I WANT A TURNAROUND.
I choose to change.
I KNOW I CAN'T CHANGE MY SPOUSE.
BUT, I CHOOSE TO EMBRACE YOUR POWER TO CHANGE ME.

FORGIVE ME.
CLEANSE ME.
REPAIR ME.

RESTORE TO US THE JOY OF FRIENDSHIP IN OUR MARRIAGE.
MAKE OUR MARRIAGE A SIGN AND A WONDER,
RATHER THAN A STATISTIC.

I KNOW THAT, WHATEVER HAPPENS,
MY FRIENDSHIP WITH YOU IS ETERNAL.
YOU ARE MY LORD AND MY SAVIOR.
YOU WILL ALWAYS BE MY VERY BEST FRIEND.
I am eternally Yours.

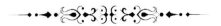

Safety

Open and Unafraid to Be Yourself
Emotionally Safe and Vulnerable with Your Spouse
Physically Protected from Violence or Harm
Your Home and Relationship Is a Place of Refuge
Together, You Are Sheltered from Storms of Life
Security in Your Relationship with God and Your Spouse
At Home in the Arms of the One You Love

Trait 3
Safety

—◆—◆—◆··◈⟨⟨⟨⟩⟩⟩◈··◆—◆—◆—

    Sitting in the back of the room observing a marriage conference led by Joe Beam, I was struck by a simple concept he shared: safety. He used a simple drawing of a brick wall to illustrate the need for safety in marriage. He talked about how walls go up between spouses when one or both feel threatened or unsafe for any reason.

    As a bestselling author of books on marriages and founder of *Marriage Helper Inc.*, Joe and his team have an impressive success rate for helping troubled marriages. And at the seminar that day, it was easy to see how the environment of safety he'd created made it possible for spouses to reconnect.

    Listening to Beam talk, I realized that, although I felt safe to openly share how I felt with my husband, Wayne didn't feel the same safety with me. Wayne processes his emotions and thoughts internally, and when he doesn't feel safe, he keeps to himself. At the seminar that day, I finally understood that every time I spoke critically of my husband, in effect, I added another brick to the wall that divided us. We had been through a couple of hard years and the bricks were stacking up between us. The taller that protective wall got, the more effectively it hindered our emotional intimacy.

When I apologized, the bricks started coming down. As I began to ask questions more consistently and draw Wayne out through listening, he openly shared his heart with me. Fresh intimacy was restored between us.

Is a Brick Wall Dividing Your Marriage?

God created each of us with hearts that desire to be open. It takes emotional energy to keep thoughts and feelings hidden. When we feel frustrated or hurt, a common response is to shut down emotionally—to protect, rather than share our hearts. To experience intimacy in marriage, both partners need to feel safe. That means your home needs to be a place of safety, a space where you are able to relax and open your hearts to each other.

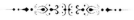

To experience intimacy in marriage, both partners need to feel safe.

When I accepted the responsibility for my actions and asked for Wayne's forgiveness, the wall between us immediately began to come down. A newly created environment of emotional safety allowed us to draw together with greater intimacy.

If an emotional brick wall is dividing your relationship, one or both of you are probably experiencing some of the following things:

- Communication is closed or strained.

- It feels as if you're walking on eggshells in an attempt to avoid confrontation.

- You feel like you have to perform a certain way to please the other person.

- There's an inability to be fully open and honest.

In addition, one or both of you may feel:

- Judged
- Disrespected
- Misunderstood or rejected
- Alone
- Mistrusted or mistrusting
- Insecure
- Uncomfortable
- Emotionally shut down

An emotionally safe marriage is one that allows you the freedom to be who you really are. You can trust that your spouse will love you no matter what. You feel unconditional acceptance. You feel safe to share the most valuable part of you—your heart. In an emotionally safe relationship, you are confident your spouse will not crush your hopes, dreams, or deepest desires. And you feel confident that what you share will remain private.

Both spouses need to embrace their responsibility to create an environment of emotional safety in their home. You can start by learning how to handle conflict in a way that builds up, rather than tears down, your partner's confidence and security.

Repairing the Breach, Restoring Your Home

Ironically, conflicts that create tension and make a marriage feel unsafe can also open a doorway to greater intimacy. Disagreements can either cause hurt and frustration or, if handled in a healthy way, create deeper connection. If you never have disagreements in your marriage, then one of the partners is not being completely honest. The arguments you have with your spouse can lead to a deeper level of honest understanding of how your spouse really thinks, feels, and views the world around him or her. The key is to keep communication open, honest, and respectful.

One of my husband's favorite Scriptures offers a beautiful picture of how God can rebuild our relationships:

The Lord will guide you continually, giving you
water when you are dry and restoring your strength.
You will be like a well-watered garden, like an ever-
flowing spring. Some of you will rebuild the deserted
ruins of your cities. Then you will be known as a
rebuilder of walls and a restorer of homes.
Isaiah 58:11–12 (NLT)

You don't want emotional walls to separate you from your spouse; you need walls of safety to surround your relationship. You repair the breach in your marriage as you rebuild the safety in your home.

Reframing Issues

The next time you enter into a disagreement, take charge of your thoughts. Instead of thinking, "He never understands me," or "She never really listens to me," intentionally place this thoughtful prayer in your mind:

God, I choose to be thankful for my spouse's per-
spective. I know that I am not always right.
Help me to honestly hear what my spouse is saying.
Keep my lips from speaking defensive comments
that will hurt. Open my heart to receive my spouse's
perspective, with greater understanding. I choose to
value my spouse's heart and guard our intimacy.

I know, in the heat of the battle, you won't be able to keep all of these words in your mind. That's why it's important to meditate on them and ask God to prepare your heart *now*—before conflict arises. The attitude with which you approach your marriage, including the conflicts, can help you speak, listen, and receive communication in a healthy and helpful way. Keeping your heart open provides the opportunity for greater intimacy.

One attitude that will help your spouse feel safe is truly valuing who he or she is as a human being. Make a commitment to never attack your spouse's character, the essence of who they are.

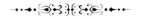

Keeping your heart open provides the opportunity for greater intimacy.

Remember, your spouse has been created in the image of God (Genesis 1:27). Fearfully and wonderfully made (Psalm 139:14), your spouse is not only your most treasured gift from God, but one of God's treasured possessions (Exodus 19:5). As you work to resolve conflict, reframing the situation—intentionally remembering that your spouse's innate value comes from God—will help prevent yourself from making hurtful comments.

Recovering from an
Adulterous Attack Against Your Marriage

In our time in ministry, Wayne and I have worked with many couples as they've tried to recover from the ravages of sexual infidelity. Adulterous attacks on marriage come in many forms, including emotional or physical infidelity, sexual addiction, and pornography. In each of these situations, please know, though difficult, recovery and restoration is possible.

Extramarital affairs break the foundation of trust in a marriage. The deceit of emotional or physical adultery leaves the spouse who has been cheated on reeling, wondering if his or her marriage—or entire life—is a lie. And it isn't uncommon for any remaining shards of trust to be completely shattered when the one who has committed the sexual offense tries to cover up the adulterous relationship by telling more lies such as, "It was only a one-night stand. She doesn't mean anything to me." When it becomes obvious this adulterous relationship is much more than a one-time mistake, the hurt spouse wonders, "How can I ever trust you again?"

Sometimes, the adulterous partner in a sexual relationship is pornography. Because of the deceptive nature of pornography, the user falsely believes he isn't hurting anyone. While it may seem harmless because another person isn't involved, pornography can be just as damaging as a "real-life" affair. At a minimum, pornography use can dampen a man's desire for sex with his spouse because real women will never look like the digitally perfected images created for magazines and websites. At its worst, pornography use can become an insatiable addiction with the power to destroy lives.

Pornography taps into the brain as a need and can become an addiction. Just like every addiction, sexual addictions can't be fully satisfied. The user feels an ever increasing need for perverted pleasure. Pornography is a $13 billion industry.[3] Its producers' primary goal is to keep people, specifically men, returning for more. Expert sales and marketing teams are employed to tempt people with the promise of pleasure—continually increasing the intensity of the perversion to draw in loyal (aka addicted) customers. The need for increasingly destructive and perverted images replaces the addict's appetite for healthy sexual pleasure. What may have begun with lust-filled fantasy and masturbation can turn into pornographic pictures that become idolatrous, unrealistic images seared on the mind. In worst case scenarios, because of the addictive nature, pornography can lead to encounters with prostitutes or one-night stands, in an attempt to satiate the addict's physical or emotional desires.

Recovering from an adulterous attack on your marriage, regardless of the form it takes, requires change in both partners. Your marriage covenant has been broken, but God can restore your relationship if both marriage partners are willing to take responsibility for their own parts in both the initiating problems and the solution.

The adulterous relationship is a symptom of the gap of an emotional, physical, and spiritual relationship between marriage partners. A strong, consistent sexual relationship is important

---

[3] "Pornography Statistics: Annual Report 2015." Covenant Eyes. (Accessed June 1, 2015). http://www.covenanteyes.com/pornstats/

for every marriage. A lack of sexual fulfillment can make marriage partners vulnerable to temptation. In a similar way, a fulfilling intimate emotional bond

→·•→·⊰⊱·3⟩⟨⊱·⊰·⊱→·•→·←

With God, anything is possible.

→·•→·⊰⊱·3⟩⟨⊱·⊰·⊱→·•→·←

is equally important. If either spouse goes underground with the essential part of who they are, the marriage is vulnerable to attack. In cases where the adulterous relationship was not only a sexual but also an emotional affair, the person who has entered the adulterous relationship may say things like, "I was able to be completely honest with her. She understands who I am," or "I felt safe with him; he didn't judge me."

Like any sin issue, sexual sin must not be allowed to continue. Jesus said,

> *If your hand causes you to sin, cut it off. It's better*
> *to enter eternal life with only one hand than to go*
> *into the unquenchable fires of hell with two hands.*
> Mark 9:42 (NLT)

With sexual infidelity of any sort, after admission of guilt, the first step is to stop all adulterous behavior. It is not appropriate or healthy for the spouse who strayed to continue in a relationship of any kind with the person with whom the affair occurred. Likewise, if there is to be healing, pornography use must completely end. Repentance means to stop going in a sinful direction and turn toward Jesus and the healing path He wants for you to take. This path can eventually lead back to a healthy sexual relationship with your spouse. With God, *anything*—even the restoration of broken marriages—is possible.

If your marriage has been breached by pornography, sexual addiction, adultery, or perversion in any way, seek professional Christian counseling. Invest the time, money, and emotional energy to find freedom, help, and hope.

Your Heart Is Key to Your Marriage

God's plan and purpose for your marriage is that you overcome all adversity through His strength. As your heart finds safety in Jesus, He will teach you how to bring safety into your marriage. The Holy Spirit is your comforter and your guide.

In a marriage covenant, you are promising before God and witnesses that you are going to be faithful and true to your spouse, sexually, emotionally, and spiritually. Keeping your relationship strong in all three of these areas creates a wholehearted connection that helps divorce-proof your marriage. In contrast, a marriage without the safety of a wholehearted connection will fail unless the bond of intimacy is restored.

Remember, if you are brokenhearted, God is able to mend your broken heart. If you feel half-hearted because of stress, hurt feelings, or broken promises, God is able to light a fresh fire of intimacy and make your relationship whole. If you or your spouse has spoken heartless words or done heartless things to each other, know that God still works miracles in the lives of couples who trust Him to restore their marriages.

You can't control what your spouse does; you can only control how you react. You can control your own choices, so choose to walk with a faith-filled perspective towards your marriage.

God is at work in your heart and in your marriage. If you have been going your separate ways, turn around, and get reconnected. If your marriage has been under attack, get help. Sometimes reinforcements are necessary for the battle to win back your relationship and rebuild a wall of safety around it. If you feel alone in your marriage, begin again to prioritize the emotional, sexual, and spiritual oneness in your relationship.

Walk with your whole heart towards God and put your marriage in His hands. Listen to His quiet whisper. Walk in purity of heart and mind. When you keep your own heart right with God, you will be ready to share your whole heart with your spouse.

—◆—◆·❧✧ʒ⟨⟩✧❧·◆—◆—

Life-Giving God,

RULER OF THE UNIVERSE,
YOU HAVE MADE THE EARTH, THE LAND AND THE SEA.
YOU ARE ALWAYS WITH ME.
YOU KNOW MY WAKING UP AND MY LAYING DOWN.
YOU KNOW MY DEEPEST AND MOST HIDDEN DESIRES OF MY HEART.
YOU WOVE ME TOGETHER IN MY MOTHER'S WOMB
AND MADE ME WHO I AM.

FIRST OF ALL, LOVER OF ALL LOVES,
I COMMIT TO KEEP YOU AS THE LOVE ABOVE EVERY OTHER LOVE.
I TURN AWAY FROM EVERY RIVAL THRONE
THAT HAS TAKEN UP RESIDENCE IN MY HOME.
CLEANSE ME. PURIFY ME. MAKE ME NEW.

I choose to share everything with You.

I'M NOT GOING TO HOLD ANYTHING BACK.
I KNOW THAT WHEN I SHARE THE MOST HIDDEN THINGS WITH YOU,
YOU ALREADY KNOW—BECAUSE YOU ARE GOD.

CREATE WITHIN MY HEART A SAFE PLACE TO BE WITH YOU.
WHEN I FEEL MISUNDERSTOOD BY MY SPOUSE, I WILL RUN TO YOU.
WHEN I FEEL HURT, WOUNDED, AND REJECTED,
I WILL COME TO YOU.
YOU ARE MY HEALER.

You are my Hope.

TODAY, I PLACE MY MARRIAGE IN YOUR HANDS.
HELP ME SEE WHERE THE ENEMY HAS DIVIDED OUR RELATIONSHIP.
I CHOOSE TO CLOSE THE DOOR OF SIN IN MY OWN LIFE.
I CHOOSE TO FORGIVE THE SIN IN MY SPOUSE'S LIFE.

GOD, DO A MIRACLE TRANSFORMATION.
BEGIN IN MY HEART AND MOVE TO MY MARRIAGE.
I TRUST YOU. I BELIEVE YOU.
YOU WILL NEVER LEAVE ME NOR FORSAKE ME.

You are my safety.

—◆—◆·❧✧ʒ⟨⟩✧❧·◆—◆—

Honesty

Sincerity and Candor Spoken with Love
Direct Open Conversation Shared Mutually
Truth-Filled Words Spoken with Respect
Transparency, Allowing God's Light to Shine
Honorable Integrity, Lived Out in Daily Life
Trustworthy and Dependable Character
Real Marriage, Dealing with Real Problems
Purity of Heart, Shared with Sensitivity

Trait 4
Honesty

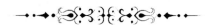

"Not another word..."

I had clearly heard God's gentle whisper, His prompting to keep my mouth shut.

But I ignored it. I wanted to say just four little words to prove my point... "I'm just being honest."

I should have listened to God. Those four words—as true as they were—ignited like gasoline on hot embers. Our disagreement immediately shifted from a minor battle into a full-blown war.

Anger, disappointment, and hurt crossed Wayne's face as he heard my words. He threw up his hands and turned around in frustration. For the first time in our relationship, he got in the car and went for a drive to cool off.

As I watched him drive away, anger and fear swelled within me. I tried to comfort myself by repeating the thought, *I was just being honest.* But, really, my words weren't so much about honesty as they were about being right. I thought being right justified my words and actions. I didn't mean to put on pride as I dressed each day, but I guess the residue from my past still clung to me. You see, I grew up in a family of debaters. We knew how to use words to win.

Do you think you are always right? Have you ever noticed that you can have the facts correct but still be completely wrong when it comes to your relationship?

Stopping the Flood

During Dr. John Gottman's research in the "love lab," he and his team noticed a repeated physiological phenomenon in couples that they labeled as "flooding." Flooding occurs when your body goes into fight-or-flight mode; it's a physical response to what is perceived as a harmful event.

The body's autonomic nervous system controls heart rate, digestion, respiratory rate, etc. During an emotional argument, a chain reaction can occur in which cortisol is released into the body, causing both blood pressure and energy levels to quickly rise. At the same time, adrenaline surges into the bloodstream and enhances physical strength. This flood of hormones is what makes it possible for ordinary people to do extraordinary things during moments of crisis.

When you are caught in this emotional flood and physiological response, you can run faster and lift more than normal. You can also hurt others more because these hormones impair your ability to think or communicate clearly. Interestingly, your body responds to threats and stress the same way—whether the "attack" is truly dangerous or is only an attack on your pride. During flooding, you may feel any combination of the following:

- Your spouse feels like "the enemy."
- You feel confused.
- You feel defensive.
- You are sweating.
- Your heart races.
- You find yourself holding your breath.
- You are unable to listen to your partner.
- You feel shell-shocked.
- You feel attacked.

Wayne and I didn't know the term or dynamic of "flooding" when we had the argument I mentioned at the beginning of this chapter. Thankfully, Wayne had the wisdom to walk away until he and I could talk things out in a self-controlled manner. While we were in the middle of this argument, he recognized that nothing he could say would make it any better. His emotions were too flooded in the moment to say anything helpful. He needed to take a break, so he took a drive and cooled down.

In your own relationship, when you or your spouse feels flooded by emotion, one of the best things you can do is say, "Let's stop for now and talk about this later." Simply being aware of the physiology of your body during an argument will help you maintain self-control with your words and actions.

Self-control is God's work in our lives. It isn't something we, as Christians, have to muster up in our own will. Self-control is a fruit that grows when we invite the Holy Spirit in to direct our lives and heed His instruction. If you think you have to do life all on your own, you may get discouraged. But when you and I realize that we have God within us to guide us in a godly response to conflict, we can listen for and lean into His strength. Prayer is an important part of leaning into God's strength.

While Wayne drove, he prayed. Not long after he left, the Holy Spirit convicted my heart. I knew I was wrong and asked for God's forgiveness. By the time Wayne returned, the atmosphere of our home had dramatically changed. He walked in to, "I'm sorry," to which he responded, "Me, too." With softer hearts and cooler heads, we worked things out. More importantly, we acknowledged that what had seemed intensely important in the moment was insignificant, compared to the joy and beauty of a long-term, loving relationship.

To this day, I can't remember what we were fighting about. If Wayne had left and we never resolved the issue, but instead pushed the conflict under the surface, that wouldn't have been healthy or helpful. In fact, left unresolved, I bet we would still remember the issue in great detail and continue to tend embers from that conflict.

The honest truth is that our relationship is more important than who is right. The measure of right or wrong goes much deeper than factual evidence. It goes to the deep places of the heart.

Ground Rules for Honesty in a Marriage

At the heart of every life-giving marriage is the trait of honesty. Since we have learned together that we don't want to trigger a negative, emotional response—even by "just being honest"— it is healthy to set some ground rules for honesty in marriage. Here are some helpful things to remember:

1. Watch Your Words

Do you hear words coming out of your mouth that you don't really mean or that you wish you could take back? Your mouth is the rudder on the ship of your life. If you aimlessly sail through life saying whatever comes to mind, you are headed for a shipwreck. You will lose friends and loved ones who get hurt by the carelessness of your tongue. True honesty is not the same as vomiting out toxic words. Honesty is tempered by the integrity of wisdom.

Have you ever noticed that if you just allow the dust to settle, what you felt intensely in the moment dims into a more balanced perspective? With the help of the Holy Spirit, you can watch your words. The power of your words is clearly described in Scripture:

> *Indeed, we all make many mistakes. For if we*
> *could control our tongues, we would be perfect and*
> *could also control ourselves in every other way...*
>
> *But a tiny spark can set a great forest on fire. And*
> *among all the parts of the body, the tongue is a*
> *flame of fire. It is a whole world of wickedness,*
> *corrupting your entire body. It can set your whole*
> *life on fire, for it is set on fire by hell itself.*
> James 3:2, 5-6 (NLT)

The tongue can be "set on fire by hell itself." Let those powerful words put into perspective which side of the argument you want to be on. We want to be on God's side and our spouse's side. Our spouse is not the enemy.

2. Listen Attentively

A bedrock condition for every marriage is mutual respect. No one is ever *completely right* in an argument. Acknowledge that it's okay to disagree. The truth is that, if both of you are in *complete agreement* about every detail, it's very likely one of you is not being honest.

Honesty is tempered by the integrity of wisdom.

Take time to listen to your spouse. Agree that one person will speak at a time. Commit to being supportive and encouraging as you listen. Be willing to listen to your spouse's place of pain. Make sure your partner feels validated by giving him or her your full attention.

Another factor of good communication is keeping your body language open and receptive. Do not try to control him or her with your body language. You know what it is like to glare at your spouse when he comes in the door. Rather than being greeted with warmth, you are the ice queen. Or have you ever been in an argument, your spouse reaches out to touch you, and you pull away? You are well able to let your spouse know how angry or disappointed you feel without speaking a word.

When you're tempted to use your body language to cut down your spouse, imagine if that was God's response to you. An ice-filled glare does not come from the God who loves us. Take charge of your emotions by controlling your thoughts. Try listening not only to the words that your spouse is saying, but to the heart behind his or her words.

Conflicts can often be soothed, if not completely resolved, with the simple act of listening. Many times, we just need to feel heard. And, in every conflict, truly listening will improve your odds of understanding your spouse.

3. Speak Honestly

Marriage should not be a series of debates in which one of you wins and the other loses. The goal is resolution and affirmation of your partnership, not forcing the other person into complete submission or agreement. In short, resolving conflict isn't about winning. It's about communicating honestly from your heart.

With that in mind, it's important to speak honestly *without* attacking the other person's character. Let love, rather than pride, measure your words. Limit your comments to the topic at hand; don't bring up past conflict or hurts.

> *[Love] does not dishonor others, it is not self-seeking,*
> *It is not easily angered; it keeps no record of wrongs.*
> 1 Corinthians 13:5 (NLT)

Since you don't have a corner on truth, no matter how convinced you are that you are right, consider what the other person has said before you open your mouth. Only then, speak the truth in love allowing Jesus, the Truth-Giver, to lead the conversation.

> *God wants us to grow up, to know the whole truth*
> *and tell it in love—like Christ in everything. We*
> *take our lead from Christ, who is the source of*
> *everything we do. He keeps us in step with each*
> *other. His very breath and blood flow through us,*
> *nourishing us so that we will grow up healthy in*
> *God, robust in love.*
> Ephesians 4:15-16 (MSG)

Part of growing up is walking humbly with the knowledge that, on a regular basis, you are wrong. Even when your intentions are right, your perspective can easily be tainted by pride and twisted by deception. The way we know the whole truth is to know Jesus. He is the source of everything. As you keep in step with Christ, the truth that comes out of your mouth won't be exaggerated. Although Scripture should be the foundation of what you believe as a Christian, do not use Scripture to prove a point. It is the Holy Spirit's responsibility to convict each one of us of sin. You are not the Holy Spirit. As you speak, listen to the Holy Spirit. Then, God's Spirit will be able to convict you both and guide you to a resolution.

4. Keep a Positive Perspective

When you are married, it is easy to spot recurring cycles in your relationship and in your spouse's behavior. What may be obvious to you could be a blind spot for your spouse and vice versa. You can slow or stop those negative cycles by maintaining a positive perspective. How? Understand that the battlefield is in your mind. If you are dwelling on the negatives surrounding your spouse, it will be magnified in your mind.

- Don't assume your spouse intended to hurt you. Give him or her the benefit of the doubt. Choose not to see his or her behavior or words as an attack.

- Just as it's important to use positive words to speak about your spouse, it's also critical to use positive words to *think* about your spouse.

- Allow your partner to grow and change. Your relationship is unfolding. There may be things that he or she thought and felt at one point in your relationship that have changed through life experience.

- Remember who you are in Christ. When you are secure in who you are, you do not need to prove yourself. This empowers you to respect the other person and hear what he or she has to say.

Keep Anger on a Short Leash

Anger in itself is not right or wrong. Jesus showed us how to be angry and not sin. But anger is a gateway to the emotional flooding we talked about earlier.

> *"In your anger do not sin": Do not let the sun go down while*
> *you are still angry, and do not give the devil a foothold.*
> Ephesians 4:26-27 (NIV)

You give anger a foothold when you act out of your flooded emotions. It is like opening the door of your home and your heart to the devil and all of his demons and saying, "Come on in." When you feel angry, it is your responsibility to close the door to that anger. Often, forgiving your spouse is the key that locks the door securely.

Do not take the phrase, "Do not let the sun go down while you are still angry" literally. This verse is really warning us against allowing anger to fester into bitterness. Unfortunately, too many couples misunderstand the spirit of this verse and stay up all night long, fighting. In such situations, fatigue works against us and makes the conflict seem much worse than it really is. Call a time-out. Get some rest. (During your time-out, be intentional about thinking positively about your spouse and your relationship. Don't use the time to amass verbal ammunition!) The light of a new day may help you resolve the conflict.

By guarding the doorway of your heart, you prevent the enemy from gaining a foothold. Your mind and heart will be at peace. You won't feel an urgency to fix things. You will be at ease knowing that the Holy Spirit is your peace-filled guide.

Honesty Bonds You to Your Spouse

One of the deepest, human desires is to be known. That means your spouse *wants* to be honest with you. But if your partner doesn't feel able to share his or her heart without fearing some sort of outburst from you, honesty won't come easily—if at all. Similarly, if your spouse fears that you will abuse his or her authenticity to manipulate or control him or her, he or she won't be honest.

Honesty grows best in an accepting atmosphere of love and respect. Honesty helps you gain ground in living life openly and transparently with your best friend.

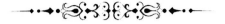

Lord Jesus,
YOU KNOW EVERYTHING.
YOU KNOW THE DEPTHS OF WHO I AM.
YOU KNOW MY FAULTS
AND YOU STILL LOVE ME.
YOU KNOW MY WEAKNESSES
AND YOU COVER ME.
YOU KNOW MY FAILURES
AND YOU, DAILY, GIVE ME A FRESH START.

I WANT TO BE LIKE YOU.
HELP ME TO LIVE A LIFE OF INTEGRITY WITH MY SPOUSE.
HELP ME TO BE OPEN AND HONEST,
UNAFRAID TO SHARE MYSELF.
Open my eyes to see from Your perspective.
OPEN MY EARS TO HEAR YOUR SPIRIT'S VOICE.
OPEN MY PERSPECTIVE
TO EMBRACE YOUR HUMILITY.

CLOTHE ME WITH YOUR CHARACTER.
YOU WERE ALWAYS HONEST,
BUT NOT CONDEMNING.
YOU SHARED TRUTH
THAT SETS EACH ONE FREE.
I trust You, Lord,
TO HELP ME DO THE SAME
WITH MY SPOUSE.
IN LOVING SURRENDER,
AMEN.

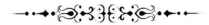

Intimacy

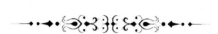

Exceptional Connection between You and Your Spouse
Affectionate Friendship and Pleasure in Each Other's Company
Extraordinary Passion for the Purposes and Plans of God
Unequaled Significance of Your Spouse
Unrivaled Commitment to Your Marriage
Incomparable Ecstasy of Being One in Marriage
Harmonious Jubilation Over Shared Love
Unparalleled Closeness with God and Each Other

TRAIT 5
Intimacy

—•→•·❦⟨⟩❦·•←•—

After my husband, Wayne, and I had been courting for some time, my father asked, "Can Wayne handle Sue?"

My father loved me dearly and always encouraged me to be strong and follow my purpose and calling. When I was a young woman, he told me, "You're just like me. You have the drive and the leadership to succeed." Even though he had three sons and I was the youngest daughter, he recognized that I possessed leadership gifts similar to those he had used to build six successful businesses.

He also recognized that my strong personality could easily overpower Wayne's calm and gentle nature. Dad's question grew out of the cultural expectation of his day that a man needed to *handle* a woman.

After many years of a satisfying intimate relationship with Wayne, I have come to understand that, if I had married a man who tried to control me by force, I would have shriveled up and died. That may sound dramatic, but I know in my heart that such a relationship would have crushed my spirit. I needed a man who was gentle, kind, trustworthy, true, and hardworking. God knew I needed a man I could trust and respect enough to surrender myself to his leadership in my life. More specifically, God knew I needed Wayne, a man who would embrace my personality without smothering, containing, or controlling me.

In a similar but opposite way, God knew that my strengths would be a blessing to my husband. I support him in his endeavors and challenge him to be all he is called to be. Together, we balance each other.

For true intimacy, each of us needs God's perspective to see our spouses as God made them to be. This bond of connection grows in an environment where we can be who God intended us to be and where our personhood is valued and our uniqueness cherished. Although acceptance of our differences is critical, for intimacy to thrive, we must be joined together by the Holy Spirit and believe we are better together than apart.

Love and Respect

Intimacy flourishes in an environment of love and respect; it shrinks in a power struggle. Intimacy so values what the other spouse brings to the marriage that each partner is willing to yield. This concept is beautifully illustrated in Scripture:

> *And further, **submit to one another out of reverence for Christ**. For wives, this means submit to your husbands as to the Lord. For a husband is the head of his wife as Christ is the head of the church. He is the Savior of his body, the church.*
> Ephesians 5:21-23 (NLT, emphasis added)

It is out of *reverence to Christ* that husbands and wives submit to one another. While essential to the context of the apostle Paul's message, these verses are often omitted in sermons about the marital relationship. The focus tends to be on the next part of the same passage.

> *As the church submits to Christ, so you wives should submit to your husbands in everything. For husbands, this means love your wives, just as Christ loved the church. He gave up his life for her to make her holy and clean, washed by the cleansing of God's word. He did this to present her to himself as a glorious church without a spot or wrinkle or any other blemish. Instead, she will be holy and without*

*fault. In the same way, husbands ought to love their
wives as they love their own bodies. For a man who
loves his wife actually shows love for himself.*
Ephesians 5:24-28 (NLT)

The apostle Paul, inspired by the Holy Spirit, tells wives to surrender (submit) to their husbands in everything. That means you yield to your husband's leadership in your life. You bring all of your life into direct relationship with your husband. You don't live independently; you are now *one* with your husband.

As wives, we are called to esteem, value, respect, and honor our husbands out of our reverence for Christ. Admiration for one's husband is not founded on how he performs as a provider, friend, or lover. Respect is not based on accomplishment, but on faith in God. That means showing love and respect even when our husbands fall short of Christ's perfection. Likewise, our husbands are commanded to love us even when we fall short of God's call to be *without spot or wrinkle.*

Husbands have the harder challenge. You are to love your wife like Jesus loved the church. In other words, you are to surrender and die to your own agenda. Being the head of your wife isn't about getting *your* will done, but seeing that *God's will* is done in your home. This perspective takes the opposite of Archie Bunker's approach, when he claimed his favorite chair in the home he called his castle on the 1970s sitcom *All in the Family.* Archie expected Edith to serve him. Christ calls the husbands to serve their wives.

As a husband, you have the weight and responsibility to cultivate the garden of your wife's emotional, spiritual, and physical needs. If you nurture her by living out the wonder of God's Word in your house, you build on Christ's foundation of holiness in your home. If you love your wife, you love yourself.

*No one hates his own body but feeds and cares for
it, just as Christ cares for the church. And we are
members of his body. As the Scriptures say, "A
man leaves his father and mother and is joined to
his wife, and the two are united into one." This is
a great mystery, but it is an illustration of the way*

*Christ and the church are one. So again I say each
man must love his wife as he loves himself, and the
wife must respect her husband.*
Ephesians 5:29-33 (NLT)

The great mystery is the beauty of oneness in marriage. The miracle is that God takes an imperfect husband and an imperfect wife and makes them one flesh. And it's about so much more than physical oneness. The culture of intimacy grows vibrant and fruitful in a marriage that is fully surrendered to Jesus and *His* ways. It is when we surrender to one another and to God that the power of the Holy Spirit unifies two very different people—making them one in Christ.

Vive la Différence

Long live the difference between men and women! Uniquely designed by the Creator, men and women are different. Not only are you a different gender from your spouse, each of you is one of a kind.

Understanding and respecting your differences will help you grow closer to your mate. You will diminish your frustration and disappointment when you are able to better understand your husband or wife.

Not only do you communicate differently; you think and behave differently. You react to stress differently, and you have different emotional, spiritual, and physical needs. Gaining insight into your differences will help you to be more loving and forgiving when your spouse doesn't respond the way you think he or she should.

Dr. Gary and Barbara Rosberg, authors of *The 5 Sex Needs of Men and Women,* researched the five top needs of a woman and compared it to the top five needs of a man. The chart on the next page summarizes their findings.

TOP 5 NEEDS OF A WOMAN	TOP 5 NEEDS OF A MAN
1. Affirmation: A wife needs affirmation. An affirming husband helps to build her self-esteem. When a wife feels good about herself, she is more likely to feel free to share herself with her husband.	**1. Mutual Satisfaction:** The purpose of mutually satisfying sex is not just orgasm, but satisfaction through an emotional and spiritual connection and mutual satisfaction of both the husband and wife.
2. Connection: A wife desires genuine connection. When a husband connects with his wife emotionally and spiritually, he prepares her for sexual intimacy.	**2. Connection:** Men desire to be understood, listened to, accepted, cared for, encouraged, and given attention.
3. Non-Sexual Touch: Daily non-sexual touch refuels a wife's energy and creates a place of safety through tender affection, with no strings attached.	**3. Responsiveness:** Responding to a husband's sexual advances will build his sexual confidence and make him more tender and attentive.
4. Spiritual Intimacy: Spiritual intimacy lights the fire of passion in a wife. Mutual heartfelt desire to be close to God fosters mutual satisfaction and intimate connection. Spending time in prayer together as a couple can be a gateway.	**4. Initiation:** Men love spontaneity. A husband needs his wife to initiate so he knows he's not the only one who cares about their sex life. When she initiates sex, he realizes that she cares about his needs, loves him, and thinks about him.
5. Romance: Romance for most women means spending quality time together. Romance is the bridge between love and sex, so when a wife's need for romance is not met, she struggles to move toward sex.	**5. Affirmation:** Only a wife can get to the most sensitive, deep, vulnerable, intimate part of a man. Only his wife can affirm him sexually.

Summarized from *The 5 Sex Needs of Men and Women* by Dr. Gary and Barbara Rosberg. Tyndale House, 2007.

It's helpful to understand the top five needs for men and women identified by the Rosbergs' research. However, you and your spouse won't necessarily fit neatly inside these boxes in the same order. In fact, each husband and wife's unique needs may change during the course of their marriage. My point in highlighting these needs is to help make each of you sensitive to your call to care for your spouse's needs. Though you will not be able to meet every need, understanding them will help you communicate more effectively and love more deeply. And as you listen and grow closer to each other, you can learn to show your love in the way your mate is best able to receive it. You'll learn his or her love language.

Learning Your Mate's Language of Love

Learning to speak each other's language of love can help you keep love alive and thriving in your marriage. Gary Chapman lists the following five love languages in his popular book called *The 5 Love Languages: The Secret to Love That Lasts.*

1. Words of Affirmation

2. Quality Time

3. Receiving Gifts

4. Acts of Service

5. Physical Touch

As you think about the different emotional needs of your husband or wife, it's helpful to understand that each individual *feels love* differently.

My husband is a very practical man with a primary way of showing his love through acts of service. After being married for many years and having so many children, I have come to cherish his way of demonstrating his love to me and our family. However, when we were sharing Christmas with each other's families for the first time, I didn't understand his love language. As a young woman, deeply in love with my fiancé, I expected to find a bit of romance under the tree on Christmas. So, imagine my surprise when I unwrapped an AM/FM radio converter for my car. I was so disappointed. To me, the gift didn't represent love or romance. It was a practical gadget you'd get a friend or yourself... not the person you loved. I wondered, *Does he even care for me?*

Clearly, we spoke different love languages. Wayne had ridden in my car with me and seen my very practical need. He wanted to give me a gift that showed how much he cared about me. He even took the time to install the converter in my car. He was showing love in his language—acts of service. Unfortunately, this gift didn't translate to my love language of receiving gifts.

We've since learned to speak and listen to the other's love language. We've also learned that healthy marriages need all five of these love languages.

You need to regularly speak affirmative words to your spouse; being positive in your perspective and words helps to build up your spouse. All of us need to hear encouraging words spoken, written, and sometimes even sung. Words can either encourage or destroy intimacy.

Every couple also needs to spend quality time together. Doing something you both enjoy helps build and maintain intimacy. Learning to love what your spouse loves is great. But even if you don't like to do *everything* together, find the common ground of things you both enjoy and build it into your schedule. Don't be selfish; think of your spouse's desires.

Giving gifts is a romantic and practical part of any intimate relationship. Find a rhythm and flow to giving gifts during special occasions and making any day special. There are probably a few wives out there who don't like to

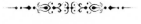

As you listen and grow closer to each other, you can learn to show your love in the way your mate is best able to receive it.

receive flowers, but I'm not one of them. I like to get flowers any time of year. Looking at a beautiful arrangement or a single blossom and smelling the sweet fragrance make me feel loved. Finding (or making) special gifts that are meaningful to your spouse shows you care about his or her likes and interests.

When you have a family, your acts of service become essential to daily life. During the pioneering days, acts of service were a part of a family's survival in the rough terrain. Now, acts of service can be as simple as doing the dishes, folding the laundry, or mowing the lawn. After many years of ministering to couples, I have learned that some women would much prefer for their husbands to show love through acts of service than buy them expensive gifts.

Physical touch is a unique language of love in a marriage. It is not only the joy of pleasuring one another during sexual intercourse; it is also the gift of touch all through the day. It can be the playful pat on the backside or the sacrificial rubbing of the feet at the end of the day. We all want and need physical touch to some degree, but learning how your spouse likes to be touched is essential to making your touch *feel* like love to the other person.

The Circle of Spiritual, Emotional, and Physical Intimacy

Learning the language of love for your spouse will require you to make yourself vulnerable and available emotionally, physically, and spiritually. These three areas are not linear with one area coming first, then second, then third. It is more like an unending circle of spiritual, emotional, and physical intimacy.

At times, I have been so angry at my husband that I didn't feel emotionally or spiritually connected. Then, seemingly out of nowhere, I would hear the Holy Spirit say, "Make love to your husband." At that moment, I didn't even want to be in the same room as him. I was mad. But when I listened to the Spirit, I found His grace. If I freely gave my heart and body to my husband, very often the spiritual and emotional aspects of our relationship fell into place.

At other times, it is the spiritual or the emotional connection that needs to come first with no pressure for sexual intercourse. Especially in a relationship in which the marriage vows have been broken, intimacy needs to be reestablished emotionally and spiritually first.

We can unlock the secrets of intimacy with our spouse by embracing God as the Holy One who created sexual oneness. Being one emotionally, spiritual, and physically creates a bond that is not easily broken. The beauty and joy of great sex as God intended strengthens this circle of intimacy. You see, God's main goal in creating sex is not for procreation or even recreation, though both are enjoyed as important parts of marriage. God's primary purpose for sex is unification—losing yourself in the ecstasy of intimately knowing and being known by your mate.

The Beauty of Redemption

No matter where you are in your marriage relationship, God has a plan of redemption for you. I don't know a couple who hasn't experienced cycles of sin in their relationship. Remember, individually and corporately, the power of this verse:

> *But if we are living in the light, as God is in the*
> *light, then we have fellowship with each other, and*
> *the blood of Jesus, his Son, cleanses us from all*
> *sin. If we claim we have no sin, we are only fooling*
> *ourselves and not living in the truth. But if we con-*
> *fess our sins to him, he is faithful and just to forgive*
> *us our sins and to cleanse us from all wickedness.*
> 1 John 1:7-9 (NLT)

Turn the light on in your relationship with God and each other. If there is any type of hidden sin in your lives, it will fight against your intimacy. You must turn the light on and cleanse your marriage from sinful patterns.

Early in our pastoral ministry, a young couple sought our counsel. The wife and husband had sought out a Christian counselor. When the husband expressed his desire to watch pornography, the "Christian" counselor encouraged them both to watch sex videos together to stimulate physical intimacy. Opening the door to pornography as a couple brought a license to sin into their home. The wife, in particular, felt dirty and devalued by this pornography. They had invited the world into their bedroom, rather than the Holy One who is the Giver of great sex. When they turned away from pornography and were cleansed from their individual sin, their home life and marital oneness were established in purity.

You may not have brought pornography into your bedroom, but are there things that you have allowed to come into your life that fight against intimacy with your spouse? If so, turn the light on. If you confess your sin to God, not only will He forgive you, but He will cleanse you and put your marital intimacy on the right track.

It takes two to be intimate. If there is only one of you working on purity in your marriage, you will face barriers that only God can remove. If you are in this situation, ask God to show you your next steps.

Be open to the leading of the Holy Spirit in your marriage. Are you supposed to spend more time together? Are you to surprise him or her with acts of service? Is there a gift you are supposed to buy to express your loyal love? Are you supposed to contact a Christian counselor to help you resolve your issues? (Remember to seek out good references and establish the integrity of his or her counsel.) Is there a marriage retreat that you should invest in? Is there a book that you are to read together? God is for you! Trust Him!

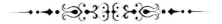

Life-Giving, Loving Father,

YOU CREATED ME TO LIVE IN INTIMACY.
YOU MADE ME TO WALK WITH OPEN AFFECTION WITH YOU.
THANK YOU FOR THE HEALTHY RELATIONSHIPS IN MY LIFE.
I KNOW THAT MY SPOUSE HAS NOT BEEN EQUIPPED BY YOU
TO MEET ALL MY NEEDS.
ONLY YOU CAN LOVE ME PERFECTLY.

Today, I choose to turn the light on in my relationship with You.

FATHER, FORGIVE ME FOR THE AREAS WHERE I HAVE
SINNED AGAINST YOU.
*(Wait for God to show you areas that
are not fully surrendered to Him.)*

I CONFESS THESE SINS TO YOU AND TRUST YOU TO
FORGIVE AND CLEANSE ME.
HELP ME TO HAVE A NEW START IN YOU.
LORD, I CANNOT CONTROL MY SPOUSE.
I FORGIVE MY SPOUSE FOR_____.

I TRUST YOU TO BRING HEALING, WHOLENESS,
AND SATISFACTION IN OUR MARRIAGE.
You are the Miracle Worker.
Redeem the broken places of our lives.
I ANCHOR MY HOPE IN YOU.
YOU ARE TOTALLY TRUE AND FAITHFUL.
I LOVE YOU, FOREVER. AMEN.

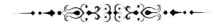

Passion

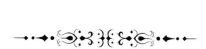

Ferocious Love for God and Each Other
Strong Emotion That Draws You Together
Hot with Desire to Be Intimate
Sexual Intimacy Is Reserved for One
Intense Arousal and Passionate Love
Intimate Affection and Friendship
Sensual Beauty and Fulfillment of Desire
Hot-Blooded Union in Marriage
Heartfelt Commitment to Serve Your Lover
Erotic Glue That Holds You Together

TRAIT 6
Passion

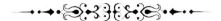

    True oneness comes from sharing oneself with another person—emotionally, spiritually, and physically. We court, fall in love, share our vows to love, honor, and cherish, and expect to live happily ever after. So when the passion Hollywood tells us should come so naturally isn't as easy as we thought it would be, disappointment can inhibit our sexual relationship with our spouse.

    I was a twenty-year-old virgin, expecting my wedding night to be magical, and, in so many ways, it was. Passionate kisses and the wonder of my husband's touch added a new dimension to the love I felt for him. But I wasn't prepared for the pain of intercourse or the emotions it brought to the surface. I felt a sense of loss, the source of which I couldn't quite pinpoint. Was it the loss of my virginity? Was it the loss of innocence? I'm not sure. What I do know is that both my new husband and I experienced a complex combination of feelings, tainted by our expectations and past experiences.

    I don't know what your wedding night was like. Nor do I know if it was the first time you had sex. I do know that the pressure we feel to create a beautiful moment can drain away the pleasure to really experience the joy of sex. So with the trepidation, excitement, passion, and pain I felt on my wedding night, I was thankful for a few of the words from a premarital seminar that we took together. I remember a man saying, "In the beginning, we weren't very good at making love." He also encouraged, "You get better at it."

The Holiness of Sexual Intimacy in Marriage •

That man was right. You get better at it. As my husband and I grew together and got to know each other physically, as well as emotionally and spiritually, we came to understand that every life-giving marriage is connected to the ultimate Life-Giver—the One who made sexual intimacy in marriage to be a holy experience.

Tim Allen Gardner explains in his book, *Sacred Sex* (WaterBrook Press), "Sex doesn't make sense unless we understand that it is holy. We can't unlock the secrets of sex and enjoy its greatest benefits unless we approach it as a holy act. Only then will couples truly experience the beauty and joy of great sex the way God intended."

God could have made procreation possible without the pleasure sensations, but He chose to create our bodies so that they are capable of orgasm. God made sexual intimacy enjoyable so that we would desire complete union—to become *one flesh*—with our mates. Even more amazing, God's nurturing power and presence is experienced powerfully in sexual union when both lovers are fully submitted to God. Gardner writes, "Sexual intimacy with all its overwhelming emotions and heart-pounding sensation was never intended to be experienced solely in the

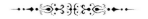

God made sexual intimacy enjoyable so that we would desire complete union—to become one flesh—with our mates.

emotional and physical realms. Rather it is to be a spiritual, even mystical, experience in which two bodies become one." When God is first in your lives, there is no hidden agenda. There are no false lovers, so you are able to be naked and unashamed.

Broken Hearts and Counterfeit Intimacy

If God created sex to be holy, why is it that, for many couples, no other topic is more painful? The creation of great sex *is* heaven born. God brought Adam and Eve together as the first husband wife and pronounced their union good. And then Satan entered the scene.

The enemy works to pervert sex and turn passion and pleasure into lust. The enemy is not able to create; he can only imitate and pervert things God has created. Satan uses our weaknesses against us by bringing up feelings of insecurity, pride, selfishness, and lust. The brokenness surrounding sexual intimacy has so many sources:

- Sexual abuse
- Sexual exploration
- Pornography
- Fear
- Loss
- Body changes
- Sexual dysfunction
- Emotional abuse
- Emotional neglect
- Lack of orgasm
- Disease
- Sexual unfaithfulness
- Emotional unfaithfulness

The list doesn't end there. You can add your own painful circumstances. While not all of these hurtful situations are the result

※※※※※

What you experience in the physical realm of your relationship will impact your emotional and spiritual relationship.

※※※※※

of sin, the enemy will use any circumstance or issue to try to pull you away from your mate and from God. He knows that women give up and give into temptation or despair if they are not sexually satisfied. Most men, whose physical needs aren't met in marriage, look elsewhere for fulfillment. Infidelity, masturbation, adultery, cybersex, and/or pornography—behaviors that may have been unthinkable before—become temptations. Like a master con man, the enemy tries to counterfeit this legitimate physical and emotional need in illegitimate ways. He knows lust is never satisfied and that no matter how you try to fulfill temptation-born lust, you will only be left with emptiness in your heart.

Unhealthy Behavior Patterns

I'm sure we had pleasurable times of lovemaking in our early marriage, but that's not what I remember most vividly. What I remember is the painful cycle of rejection and stonewalling.

After a rough beginning, I wanted our sexual relationship to be stronger. I read that men are stimulated visually, so I surprised Wayne one day by wearing new lingerie. I expected him to be thrilled and throw me on the bed. His response lacked the enthusiasm I'd hoped to see, and it crushed me. It had taken courage to offer myself that way, and it hurt to feel rejected. Angry, I gave him the silent treatment for days. I shot him looks of contempt. At night, I moved to the far side of the bed and cried into my pillow.

This wasn't a one-time occurrence. Over a period of months, we fell into a hurtful pattern of rejection and stonewalling. As the pastors at our new church, I wasn't sure who to talk to about the emotional pain and lack of sex in our marriage.

From Wayne's perspective, he couldn't do anything right. If he didn't respond the exact way I expected, he got the cold treatment. My words of criticism, contempt, and blame made him want to retreat into the comfort of his books. He wanted to be anywhere other than with me.

Why am I being so honest about this? Because, after years of working with married couples, I know relationships suffer when behavior patterns like rejection and stonewalling aren't addressed and resolved. If an unhealthy cycle of behavior is preventing you from experiencing a fulfilling sexual relationship with your spouse, you must first be honest about it and then let God heal that brokenness in your marriage.

If you are a husband who wants sex all the time but aren't aware or concerned with whether your wife has an orgasm, then let God's light shine into the selfishness that may be hidden in your heart. If you are a wife who would rather make a grocery list in your mind during sex while your husband *just does his thing,* you need to be honest about the lack of connection and passion in your marriage. If you, like many women, have trouble reaching orgasm during intercourse, you simply may not be interested in sex. But a satisfying and passionate relationship is possible. Remember, God created sex to be a holy, unifying, and pleasurable experience between a husband and wife. So don't give up! Work through the issues that threaten to steal your joy. Making love unites you as a couple—it's an act of war against the enemy who wants to tear you apart. What you experience in the physical realm of your relationship will impact your emotional and spiritual relationship.

The Healing Power of God

In 1990, our house caught fire with my newborn daughter and me inside. Trapped by smoke and flames, I was unable to get to my baby in her crib. Thankfully, my husband came home in time. He and a fireman rescued both of us from the fire. (You can read more about this event in *9 Traits of a Life-Giving Mom*).

Our marriage went from low-grade stress to over-the-top stress level. Not only were we fighting with our insurance company to pay for the damages of our home, we fought with each other *every day*. Our newborn daughter developed colic, screaming inconsolably for hours at a time. Emotionally numb, we struggled to survive each day as we stumbled through our pastoral duties. Our own need for healing, individually and as a couple, made us less effective in our ministry.

Our sex life shifted from difficult to nonexistent. As a new mother with milk-engorged breasts and an overweight body, I felt more like a feeding station than a vibrant, sensual young woman. Pregnancy and childbirth brought changes in my hormones and left painful, physical reminders that made the thought of sex completely unappealing.

The stress from fire pushed our relationship over the edge. Both Wayne and I knew we needed help if our marriage was going to work. We approached our ministry supervisor, who pointed us to a prayer-counseling ministry that included a weekend-long session. With our ten-month-old baby who was still nursing, we traveled eight hours to the event, prayerful that God would show us a solution.

Throughout the weekend, pastoral leaders shared from the heart. They were honest and candid about their own brokenness and shared how they found healing. In addition to group sessions where we heard testimonies of renewed relationships, Wayne and I received individual ministry. We met with pastoral counselors with whom we shared painful experiences in our lives. During that time of counseling and confession, we each uncovered how events from our past darkened the lens through which we viewed sex.

Years earlier, a promiscuous young woman seduced Wayne. He gave into the temptation of sex. Guilt scarred him, even though he had repented and remained celibate until we were married. He felt bound by the experience and was unable to express himself physically and emotionally like he wanted. His confession of sin and prayers of cleansing brought freedom and hope.

My own innocence was compromised by a sexually abusive situation. Although the young man never penetrated my body, the wounds of being taken advantage of left me scarred. As I talked about that event and prayed with the counselor and my husband, I felt a rush of freedom and healing when I was finally able to forgive the perpetrator.

Being honest with each other and with God allowed His light to shine into our relationship and mend our broken places. As a result, our sexual intimacy went from being the coldest part of our relationship to being hot and steamy. Adding to our newfound physical intimacy was a spiritual unity like we had never experienced in our lives. Wayne initiated a time of prayer early in the mornings before he went to his secondary job. Very often, we made love after that time of prayer together before he left for his early morning shift. The spiritual fulfillment of prayer flowed into an emotional connectedness, which lit the fire of physical intimacy.

We couldn't get enough of each other. We were truly changed. Wayne read Christian books about sexual intimacy and grew in his knowledge as a lover. He selflessly brought me so much pleasure that sex became my favorite pastime. Through subsequent pregnancies and recovery, we kept making love, continuing to nurture our emotional, spiritual, and physical relationship.

Because we understand the need for all three strands of the spiritual, emotional, and sexual aspects of marriage to be strongly entwined, we've since coached and encouraged many couples through marriage ministry. We were passionate to help and compassionate about the pain. And we know that God can heal and renew relationships in exciting and beautiful ways.

Turning Around

Whatever negative, or even life-destroying, habits you or your spouse has become entangled in, there is hope for a turn-around.

The beginning place of greater intimacy in our marriage starts with our relationship with God. When King David turned his heart back toward God after his adulterous relationship with Bathsheba, these are the words he wrote:

> *Have mercy on me, O God,*
> *because of your unfailing love.*
> *Because of your great compassion,*
> *blot out the stain of my sins.*
> *Wash me clean from my guilt.*
> *Purify me from my sin.*
> *For I recognize my rebellion;*
> *it haunts me day and night.*
> *Against you, and you alone, have I sinned;*
> *I have done what is evil in your sight....*
> Psalm 51:1-4 (NLT)

The turnaround for David began with his relationship with God. He put his hope in God. He placed his trust in God. Read his heartfelt prayer aloud:

> *Purify me from my sins, and I will be clean;*
> *wash me, and I will be whiter than snow.*
> *Oh, give me back my joy again;*
> *you have broken me,*
> *now let me rejoice.*
> *Don't keep looking at my sins.*
> *Remove the stain of my guilt.*
> *Create in me a clean heart, O God.*
> *Renew a loyal spirit within me.*
> *Do not banish me from your presence,*
> *and don't take your Holy Spirit from me.*
> *Restore to me the joy of your salvation,*
> *and make me willing to obey you.*
> Psalm 51:7-12 (NLT)

David not only had sex with another man's wife, he had her husband murdered. In his desperation, he trusted that God was the One who could purify his heart. He trusted God to give him back his joy. He trusted God to restore his life.

Lovers for a Lifetime

Today, most husbands and wives bring baggage into the marriage bed. Whether it is sexual abuse, pornography, sexual promiscuity, abortion, or any number of sexual addictions, most marriages face challenges before they even begin.

When I was engaged to Wayne, I began to have dreams recalling sexual abuse I had experienced as a child. Certain things made me feel unsafe. For instance, if Wayne scared me by surprising me from behind, I could go into a state of flight that he had no intention of triggering.

I went through counseling to help me deal with my feelings about the sexual abuse before we got married. At different points throughout our marriage, like when we had our first child, different issues have come up. Often, my dreams helped bring to light my hidden feelings.

One reason I know God hand-picked Wayne for me is the way my husband gently loved me and healed me through this process of being able to embrace my sexuality. Wayne also read book after book to increase his skill as a lover. He wanted to learn. So at night before bed, he would be reading another book about sex. It was our joke, the pastor who read sex books. Together, we learned from each book that we read.

When Two Become One, by Christopher and Rachel McClusky, is a book we appreciate and one we highly recommend to couples. One of the most helpful aspects of the book is the description of the stages of lovemaking.

PHYSICAL INTIMACY
1. Atmosphere: Intimate marriage, mature lovers, privacy, energy, time, anticipation, initiation, mutual consent.
2. Arousal: Playful vulnerability, mutual exploration, attention to the senses, letting passion build.
3. Apex: Focus on pleasure building, greater spiritual connection, abandonment to lovemaking, surrender of control, climax with no strings attached.
4. Afterglow: Restablizing, cuddling, and caressing, affirmation, reflection and basking, feedback.

When Two Become One by Christopher and Rachel McClusky. Revell, 2006.

From this book and through our own experience as marriage partners, we've discovered a few essentials for creating a physically intimate relationship:

Set an atmosphere for lovemaking in your bedroom. In one of the houses we built, we actually tried to soundproof our bedroom so that we could be unhindered in our lovemaking. Invest in your bedroom to make sure that the decor invites sexual intimacy. Do you have the candles and the candle lighter available? Are you ready with any creams, lotions, or gels that you might want to use to pleasure each other?

Pay attention to the hints from your lover. Let your arousal build when you plan for mutual exploration. Planning can be as exciting as unexpected encounters. If you set the stage for a healthy sexual relationship, you will grow in your readiness and expectation.

Make sex an open part of your marital conversation. Having a playful conversation of planning for your next sexual encounter helps make the time a priority. If you have a large family, you have to plan. Send your children to a friend's or to their grandparents' home.

Ask the Holy Spirit to lead you in making sex wonderful. Pray about what would surprise, stimulate, and excite your partner. Shake things up. Have a bubble bath running for two with something bubbly to drink. Make special foods and set them in different areas of the house. Buy fragrant massage oils. Buy a sexy nightgown. Set the mood with music, candles, and fragrance.

As you are reading this book, undoubtedly, the Holy Spirit will bring creative ideas of how you can take the area of physical intimacy to a different level. It's important not to give up on intimacy for any reason. Whether you are dealing with sexual dysfunction, or overcoming the ravages of an extramarital affair, God cares about your sex life. Bring God into the center of your love life with your spouse.

Passion Restored

If you want to experience a more passionate relationship with your spouse, first focus on restoring passion in your heart for God. God is the One who has made you. You will find the fullness of joy in Him. Restoration of passion is a daily choice to walk freely with God. Right now, make your focus be on your personal relationship with the Lover of your soul.

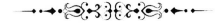

God,
I CHOOSE YOU
TO BE THE LOVER OF MY SOUL.
YOU ARE THE ONE WHO KNOWS ME THE BEST.
YOU ARE THE ONE WHO CREATED ME.
You are the One who gives my life purpose.
YOU ARE THE ONE WHO KNOWS WHEN I DRIFT AWAY FROM PASSION.

LIGHT THE COLD COALS OF MY HEART.
GO TO THE HIDDEN WOUNDS AND CLEAN MY SORE PLACES.
LOOK GENTLY AT THE UGLY THINGS HIDDEN FROM VIEW.
LIKE A SURGEON, PURIFY MY HEART.
I TRUST YOU.
I PUT MY HOPE IN YOU.
Make me fully alive in Your presence.
IGNITE ME TODAY WITH FRESH PASSION.
AMEN!

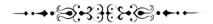

Endurance

Emotional, Physical, and Spiritual Staying Power
Willing to Walk in Consistency
Displaying Daily Patience and Persistence
Your Character Marked with Perseverance and Restraint
Resolve and Determination to Loyalty and Love
Capacity to Overcome Difficult Circumstances
Tenacity to Hold on to God's Purposes
Rock-Solid Commitment to Your Marriage

Trait 7
Endurance

The marriage relationship has a way of taking a back burner to our lives. Busyness takes over and, without even meaning to allow it, neglect creeps in while we're chasing babies, keeping track of teenagers, and earning a living. At least, that's what happened in our marriage.

Life was good. Sure, we were busy. Our family had grown to eight with four daughters and two recently adopted sons. We both served as full-time associate pastors and worked with marriages within our congregation. But amidst all the carpooling, counseling, and hurrying, we didn't realize we needed a marriage checkup ourselves.

A week before we celebrated our twenty-fifth wedding anniversary, we hosted a birthday party for our daughter, Angela. Cooking for a crew of teenagers wore me out, but, after cleaning up from the party, I couldn't sleep. I began having terrible pain in my abdomen. Then the vomiting took over. After vomiting a dozen times, I knew something was very wrong. This wasn't a normal stomach bug. I called the doctor, who confirmed I needed to head to the emergency room right away.

When we arrived at the hospital, the ER doctor quickly diagnosed acute appendicitis. While I waited to have emergency surgery, the nurse looked in my eyes and said, "Honey, I'm going to give you some morphine; I know you are in a lot of pain."

I began to cry. Tears fell, but not because of the pain. I had already endured hours of excruciating pain without crying. I cried because my pain was validated. She understood.

Instantly, I became livid with my husband. It seemed as if it had taken forever to wake him up that night. And it wasn't until the doctor told me to go to the hospital that he believed my pain was serious. Now, to be fair, Wayne's family never went to the doctor, unless it was an absolute emergency. I simply had to convince him it was an emergency. In that moment, exhausted and hurting, I was beyond frustrated that it had taken someone else to validate my pain. We lived together, for goodness' sake. Shouldn't he have been the first to see my suffering?

As the nursing staff prepped me for surgery, I looked at the surgeon and said, "Doctor, you need to do a great job because, one week from today, my husband and I are getting on a plane for Hawaii to celebrate our twenty-fifth anniversary." Even under the influence of painkillers, it was clear to me that Wayne and I had become disconnected. We *needed* some time away—just the two of us. The doctor smiled and said, "I can't make any promises."

A Stress Test for Your Marriage

Doctors use stress tests to check for hidden problems in the heart. The test is designed to see how the heart is working—how the blood flows, how it responds to exertion. If you fail your stress test, the doctor may order an angiogram to look for hidden blockages in the arteries or veins near your heart.

When I was in seminary, I served as a chaplain on the cardiac floor at a trauma hospital. I saw healthy looking patients who, only days before, were living normal lives. After these tests, they were heading into open heart surgery. Suddenly, their whole lives had been turned upside down.

Hidden neglect can block the healthy life-giving flow of your relationship. The signs of risk may not surface until stressful situations test your marriage. And, suddenly, you wonder what's happened to your relationship and why you don't know each other as well as you should, after so many years together.

We didn't think we were neglecting our marriage. We went away for a couple of days every year around our anniversary, but this was the first time we were taking an entire week together. We needed it.

Although the doctor cleared me for the trip, I got onto the plane for Hawaii in a weakened condition. Aside from the physical scar, all the emotions that spiked just before my surgery made me feel somewhat fragile. Looking back, it's easy to see how a heavy season of stress had taken its toll on our lives and our relationship. How did we come to the point where there was so much stress in our lives?

Hidden neglect can block the healthy life-giving flow of your relationship.

- We had adopted two special needs sons from Brazil. They were living in an orphanage most of their lives, until we adopted them at ages twelve and eight.

- Our daughters were reaching the upper teenage years, and we faced new challenges in parenting.

- We both worked as associate pastors at the same congregation. The church weathered tremendous stress during the downturn in the economy. Since we were both working full-time to care for others' needs, we placed our own needs on the back burner.

- Our own finances were challenging. The cost of caring for so many children was at its height. We were paying off the expensive costs of a foreign adoption.

- And for the first time in my life, my health was being challenged. I hadn't felt right physically, since returning from Brazil earlier that year.

Can you relate? If you have been married for any length of time, you likely have your own list of stress factors. It could be:

- The death of someone you loved.
- A difficult or demanding job.
- Sexual dysfunction.
- Health challenges.
- Financial challenges.
- Special needs of your children.
- Buying or selling a house.
- The list goes on and on...

Without the life-giving trait of endurance, the stress of life will ruin your once healthy marriage.

Replacing Your Stress with God-Given Endurance

Stress is the strain and pressure from life. It creates physical and mental tension in our bodies. We can be overcome with worry and anxiety. As humans, we can only bear an overload of stress of life for so long before something gives way. Like a rubber band stretched beyond its capabilities, your marriage can snap or even break.

As Christians, we don't mean to be in denial, but, sometimes, we use our faith-filled perspective to overlook the realities

The enemy attacks during times of stress, when life seems overwhelming. But Jesus promises abundant life.

of stress—a practice that may not be healthy or helpful. Rather than burying stress or pretending it doesn't exist, a better tactic is acknowledging it and looking to God as our source of relief and endurance.

The apostle Paul went through a great deal of stress in his life. He was stoned and left for dead. He was taken prisoner unjustly. He was shipwrecked. He knew what it meant to suffer, yet, while in prison, he wrote these words:

...that I may know Him and the power of His
resurrection, and the fellowship of His sufferings,
being conformed to His death....
Philippians 3:10 (NKJV)

One of the ways we get to know God is through suffering. I hate to say it, but marriage can be a crucible in which we must die to our flesh over and over again.

God intends for marriage, like a crucible, to be able to withstand high temperatures. The purifying process in your own marriage carries the precious metal of the mystery of Christ. Marriage after all, represents our relationship with Christ. All Christians, male and female, are the bride of Christ.

The enemy wants this purifying process to discourage you. He wants to destroy you and your marriage. We know from Scripture:

The thief does not come except to steal, and to kill,
and to destroy. I have come that they may have life,
and that they may have it more abundantly.
John 10:10 (NKJV)

This verse carries a warning and a promise. The warning is: Watch out! You have a very real enemy. He seeks to steal. He tries to kill. He strives to destroy. The enemy attacks during times of stress, when life seems overwhelming. But Jesus promises abundant life. Just like Jesus went through crucifixion and came out the winner, so can you!

Yes, on this earth we go through *tough* things, but it is in fellowshipping with Jesus during these times of suffering that we become more like Him. After you go through experiences where your flesh is crucified, you begin to experience the power of His resurrection in your daily life. He promises you *life*—not just that you will survive, but you will thrive. Your inheritance in Him is abundance.

I want to be careful at this point not to falsely predict that, if you are in a struggling marriage, you will not divorce. I can't control your choices. Nor can you control the choices of your spouse. I know too many people who did not want or choose a divorce, but ended up divorced nonetheless. But know this: The promise Jesus has for you is bigger than your marriage. It is a promise to you personally. No matter what happens, you can find the peace and strength to endure when you trust in Christ.

That said, this promise of abundant life does apply to our marriages as Jesus is given liberty and leadership in our lives. Jesus has defeated the enemy on the cross. The enemy may attack you, but he won't be able to win if you and your spouse commit to rely on Christ to direct your hearts, minds, and actions.

The Temptation to Blame Each Other

The Bible warns us that we will have hard times. Storms are guaranteed to hit. You may have clear skies and smooth sailing eighty percent of the time, but, for at least twenty percent of the time, storms will cause you to hold on for your very life. When your

The fantasy of the perfect, romantic marriage is perpetuated by fiction.

life is filled with stress, there is a temptation to blame your spouse. Rather than blaming one another for how tough life is, encourage each other with the hope that you can get through any circumstance. The enemy wants to divide you. Holding on to one another and clinging to Christ is how you fight against the enemy's schemes. There may be times that holding on to your marriage requires all your strength. It's during those hard times that faith has the opportunity to fuel endurance.

Faith Fuels Endurance

During stressful times and the storms of life, faith needs to be anchored in Jesus Christ. If you try to anchor your marriage on whether or not you *feel happy,* your marriage will be shipwrecked. In North America, the fantasy of the perfect, romantic marriage is perpetuated by *fiction.* Hollywood fairy tales teach us that our happiness is our spouse's responsibility. This superficial view of marriage doesn't take reality into account. Marriages founded on a fictional, happily-ever-after notion cannot stand the test of time.

Rather than happiness, what we need is faith-filled *joy.* Happiness is a fleeting feeling. Joy runs deeper than happiness. Happiness is based on your ever-changing circumstances in your life. Joy finds its source in the deep, eternal fountain that comes from God Himself. You can be filled with the joy of God even in the midst of pain. Joy is the sweetness of His presence; it overwhelms the bitter suffering that the enemy brings your way.

During your battle-filled days of endurance, let these three truths guide your perspective:

1. "This Too Shall Pass"

If the saying above seems old-fashioned, think of it as time-tested. My mom said this to me whenever I was upset about something as a girl. I have long since forgotten those temporary, teenage trials, but I remember her words of truth.

When your confidence in your marriage is not anchored on happiness but on covenant, you will anticipate that your marriage will get better. Too many times, I have seen couples who chose to divorce because they wanted to escape the pain in their lives. What they don't realize is that divorce carries with it a whole new set of trials.

Divorce severs the very fabric of a couple's existence. Every relationship in their lives is hurt by it—sometimes irreparably so. Their finances are cut in half. They deal with the stress of a divided family and divided loyalties. What seemed like an easy solution becomes a greater challenge than they could imagine. Perhaps that's why God hates divorce because He knows the pain it brings to His children when these covenant relationships are torn apart.

On the other hand, I have seen couples weather terrible circumstances and reach a loving future together. God's redeeming love is able to make the sorrows of yesterday seem fleeting.

Storms have a way of blowing over. Rely on God. Hold onto your spouse and choose to love him or her the way God loves you. Anticipate that, when you do so, the storm will pass.

2. *God Is Good*

Through every trial in your marriage, it is important to draw closer to Christ—the lover of your soul. Make Jesus the love of your life and every trial will eventually be turned into triumph. Because God is good, you can trust Him for a bright future. That means, *even if* your marriage ends in an unwanted divorce, you can trust in the goodness of God. You can trust Him to be with you through every tsunami of difficult circumstances.

God's goodness never changes. Don't try to go through it alone. Rely on Jesus for support, comfort, and strength for every step.

3. *You Are Becoming More Beautiful (or Handsome)*

Part of God's beauty treatments in our lives comes from His crucible. Some lessons can only be learned through difficult experiences. Very difficult trials are often experienced prior to God bringing beauty from ashes.

> *To all who mourn in Israel, he will give a crown*
> *of beauty for ashes, a joyous blessing instead of*
> *mourning, festive praise instead of despair. In their*
> *righteousness, they will be like great oaks that the*
> *Lord has planted for his own glory.*
> Isaiah 61:5 (NLT)

God Himself, through His redeeming love, has set up an exchange system. He replaces every ugly and life-destroying experience with life-giving beauty.

It's the same way in any type of mourning you experience in your marriage. God is able to take your mourning and turn it into dancing. He turns the heaviness of heart into joy.

How does He do it? Through the miracle of His grace. You can't earn it. You can't buy it. It has already been purchased by Jesus' blood. The joy of your salvation is not just going to heaven for eternity. Your joy begins every day as you walk fully alive in Him.

Embracing the Bitter Sweetness of Endurance

This life-giving journey we are on is not a short sprint; it's a lifelong marathon. You gain greater and greater stamina from the storms you endure.

When you think you can't get through something, trust in God's strength. Replace your fairy tale expectations with the promise-filled future of a life anchored in the power of His redeeming love. Remember that your hope and joy is not reliant on your spouse's behavior. You can't control their choices. You can't stop your husband or wife from having an affair. You can't prevent life-altering accidents or unexpected events. But you can trust Jesus to walk with you through any trial.

If you want your hope to be secure, anchor it on Christ's everlasting love. Rely on Him to help you weather hurricane force storms. He will never leave you nor forsake you. He will always be with you. Cling to Him.

You gain greater and greater stamina from the storms you endure.

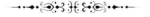

Eternal Father,
FILL ME AFRESH WITH YOUR HOPE AND PERSPECTIVE.
I HAVE BEEN TOSSED AND TURNED ON A SEA OF DOUBT.
I HAVE THOUGHT THE WORST RATHER THAN HOPED THE BEST.

CREATE IN ME A CLEAN SPIRIT, O, GOD!
FORGIVE ME AND CLEANSE ME FOR MY SIN.
WHEN I SIN AGAINST MY SPOUSE, I SIN AGAINST YOU.

Awaken within me a heart of hope.
I CHOOSE TO LIFT UP MY HEAD TO TRUST YOU.
YOU ALONE ARE TOTALLY TRUSTWORTHY AND TRUE.

ENRAPTURE ME WITH YOUR NEVER-ENDING LOVE.
SURROUND ME WITH YOUR SONGS OF DELIVERANCE.
SECURE MY HEART WITH YOUR HANDS.
I trust You.

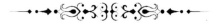

Restoration

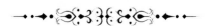

Redeeming Love, Healing You of Brokenness
Regaining Loyalty to Each Other and God
Rejuvenating Passion for Your Spouse
Rehabilitating after Loss and Growing in Trust
Repairing Relationships through the Power of the Cross
Rebuilding Intimacy with Each Other and God
Reclaiming Your Call and Purpose as a Couple

TRAIT 8
Restoration

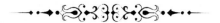

I was furious. It didn't matter that I encouraged him to go on the prayer retreat with a group of men or that I'd wanted him to experience the time of fellowship with the other men and with God. Now that he was actually gone, I felt abandoned. Wayne would be in Denver for an entire week, while I stayed home and took care of...*everything.*

We'd moved from Nashville to a suburb of Dallas, just six weeks earlier. My first book, *9 Traits of a Life-Giving Mom,* was due to release in bookstores in the next few days. I felt so small and alone in the big state of Texas.

I spent the entire first morning of Wayne's trip fuming to myself. Thoughts about how angry I felt circled endlessly in my mind. As I went about my day, I recounted all the reasons he should have stayed home, when our lives seemed so hectic. Mid-morning, feeling well and truly sorry for myself, I picked up the phone and called a friend to go out to lunch with me, so I could vent to her. Oh, I didn't exactly *plan* to vent and didn't, at first. But over dessert, with tears in my eyes, I shared my frustration with her about how hard it was to move across the country. Her comforting words fueled the fire. She understood how I felt; why couldn't my husband?

Later that day, still furious, I called Wayne to talk with him about a poor choice our sons had made in his absence. As I spoke (ranted), the real reason for my irrational rage suddenly became crystal clear to me. Wayne hadn't done anything wrong; we were under attack—smack-dab in the middle of spiritual warfare. I was in over my head. Immediately, my heart cried out to God for help.

I had experienced this type of spiritual battle in my marriage before. Looking back, I noticed a pattern of unhealthy, hurtful behaviors. Every time we were about to lead a major marriage conference, seminar, retreat, or any other event where our marriage and ministry could impact others' lives, we fell into a pain-filled cycle of rejection and quiet rage.

With a wiser perspective, I now saw that the enemy staged these attacks against us by whispering thoughts that my unchecked emotions were happy to run with. You may recognize his telltale warfare tactics. They often sound something like this:

"She ALWAYS does this…"

"He NEVER takes time to understand my needs…"

"I TOLD HIM what I needed, but he still did this…"

"She is SELFISH…"

"I'm NOT going to put up with this anymore…"

"She is never going to CHANGE…"

"If he is going to do this, then I am going to…"

Have you been in warfare like this? If you are married, I know the answer. YES! The enemy hates marriages. He uses every opportunity to divide a husband and a wife.

Walking alone in our neighborhood park later that day, I realized what I needed to do. Somewhere, I had opened a door and allowed the enemy access to my heart. I needed to seal off every door and seek refuge in Jesus.

As I sought the Lord for insight on how I'd allowed the enemy access to my heart, He showed me a petty thing that my husband had done. He had sinned against me in a small way, but the dart had nonetheless wounded my heart. Jesus also showed me a deeper

No matter who you are or how long you've been married, we all need to seek Jesus.

issue of recurring pain in my marriage. He led me to forgive my husband—completely. Then, like a skilled surgeon, He removed the enemy's arrow out of my wounded heart. He flushed out the poison of hopelessness and renewed my heart with hope. He cut away the disappointment and filled the empty space with courage.

People mistakenly assume that, if you're in ministry and/or have managed to stay married for thirty years, your life is perfect. The truth is that, no matter who you are or how long you've been married, we all need to seek Jesus.

That night, Jesus anointed my heart with the soothing oil of His presence. He closed the door to the enemy. Then He spoke to my heart:

"Sue, this oppression is from the enemy. He knows you are about to write *9 Traits of a Life-Giving Marriage.* He wants to divide you and Wayne. He wants to knock you off-center and fill you with anger and rage.

"I am going to use your pain to give you a heart of compassion for marriages. Both husbands and wives have experienced heart-wrenching disappointments from their spouses. The unspeakable pain has stolen their hope. They are discouraged. They want to give up. I am going to use you to bring boldness and courage.

"I am anointing you to be a wounded healer. I want you to *let it all hang out.* I want you to be transparent in your own pain and disappointment. Let Me shine through your transparency with the light of presence. As I have healed your heart, I will heal theirs."

Love Is War

You are in a war for your marriage. The hard part is that the enemy disguises his attacks through deceptive devices.

- The enemy distracts you from focusing time and energy on your marriage.

- The enemy uses sin in your lives to create cycles and circles of conflict.

- The enemy pours gasoline on smoldering disagreements.

- The enemy convinces you that your secret addiction will bring comfort.

- The enemy will set up situations and traps for you to fall into his pit.

- The enemy hates you and your marriage.

The enemy wins the war through your own complacency. But you don't have to let him. With God's help, you can fight against the enemy and win. You can win the victory by controlling your thoughts and deeds, learning to forgive and setting healthy boundaries, speaking and loving with truth and grace, and being willing to restore your marriage and letting God's redemption heal its broken places.

1. Thought and Deed

The battlefield for your marriage takes place in your mind. No foul deed is committed without first being conceived in the mind. The apostle Paul exhorts us to be aware of the enemy's tactics and to control our thoughts:

> *The world is unprincipled. It's dog-eat-dog out there! The world doesn't fight fair. But we don't live or fight our battles that way—never have and never will. The tools of our trade aren't for marketing or manipulation, but they are for demolishing that entire massively corrupt culture. We use our powerful God-tools for smashing warped philosophies, tearing down barriers erected against the truth of*

God, fitting every loose thought and emotion and
impulse into the structure of life shaped by Christ.
Our tools are ready at hand for clearing the ground
of every obstruction and building lives of obedience
into maturity.
2 Corinthians 10:3-6 (MSG)

Our thoughts are either tools in the hands of the enemy or tools in the hand of God. The culture of the world does not support healthy marriages. It's the culture of heaven with which we must align our thinking. Like a hammer, the act of thinking and meditating on God's Word smashes through demonic agendas for our lives. We have to actively take thoughts captive that don't agree with God's plan for our marriages. Read the following truth-filled statements. Meditate on them and speak them aloud. Saying the truth out loud allows you the ability to *hear* it too, which further strengthens your perspective of faith:

- *God strengthens me, every day, to live for Him.*
- *God is for me, so who can be against me?*
- *God is for our marriage to be healthy and life-giving.*
- *God is helping me to overcome every addiction in my life.*

With the truth in focus, let your God-centered thoughts turn into prayer.

"Jesus, I know You love _____ even more than I do. I trust
You to lead, guide, and protect _____ from harm..."

As your perspective aligns with God's truths and your thoughts become prayerful, your deeds will be more loving and less selfish. Let the Holy Spirit show you how to pray each moment of the day and be open to His prompting to serve others—especially your spouse.

2. Forgiveness and Boundaries

My husband has preached at many weddings. He often challenges the couple to memorize these words:

I was wrong. I am sorry. Please forgive me.

85

When spoken with sincerity, these words hold great power for restoring relationship in marriage. Sin separates; forgiveness repairs. Sin damages; forgiveness heals. Sin ransacks lives; forgiveness restores marriages.

Forgiving someone can be difficult—especially if the person has not apologized or asked for your forgiveness. But, as Christians, carrying unfor-

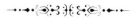

Grace is the balm that brings healing from the imperfections each spouse brings to the marriage.

giveness is not an option. God's Word commands us to forgive, just as Christ forgave us.

> *Be kind and compassionate to one another,*
> *just as in Christ God forgave you.*
> Ephesians 4:32 (NIV)

Set boundaries in your relationship and home by talking about the positive expectations for your marriage. Ban words and deeds that are toxic to you and/or your spouse. *Note:* Forgiveness does not mean that you allow abuse in your life and home. You are too precious to God to allow abusive talk or actions to scar your personhood. If physical or emotional abuse is occurring in your relationship, please seek help from a qualified Christian counselor.

3. Truth and Grace

For a marriage to be successful, it needs to be balanced with truth and grace. Jesus is described in this way:

> *And the Word became flesh and dwelt among us,*
> *and we beheld His glory, the glory as of the only*
> *begotten of the Father, full of grace and truth.*
> John 1:14 (NKJV)

Jesus not only became human, but He made His home among us. His love was unfailing. He was always faithful. He was generous, inside and out. He was genuine, truth-filled, and honest. In order for a marriage to be balanced with truth and grace, it needs Jesus at the center of it.

Truth anchors a marriage in moral conduct; it holds fast the commitment to fidelity and purity. Truth without grace, however, can be harsh, cruel, and intimidating.

Grace is the balm that brings healing from the imperfections each spouse brings to the marriage. Grace is the empowerment from the Holy Spirit to love one's spouse unconditionally. Grace without truth is like a body with no skeletal structure. Truth is the backbone that holds up the grace-giving hug.

The sweet fragrance of grace accepts, forgives, and encourages each spouse to embrace the frailty of humanity. Truth supports each spouse to be loving and loyal to the marriage covenant. Like a wedding ring, grace and truth are signs—to others and to your spouse—of your love for and commitment to each other.

4. *Restoration and Redemption*

Restoration and redemption, like truth and grace, both need to be present for a marriage to be healthy. Every husband and wife sins against his or her spouse. In fact, I believe the imperfections of humanity show up most clearly within the construct of marriage. Like the old song says, "You always hurt the ones you love, the one you shouldn't hurt at all."

Because cycles of sin are evident in human relationships, each marriage needs the empowering restoration and redemption that comes from the cross of Jesus Christ. Restoration repairs and rebuilds trust when it is compromised. Redemption is the divine exchange of our sin with God's righteousness. Jesus is the only One who can pay off the debt that each spouse owes to the other.

A friend of mine went into her marriage, filled with hope and expectation. As a virgin bride, she had kept herself pure for her husband. Both of them were good-looking, athletic, articulate, and they deeply loved each other. They made a covenant "until death do we part." In many ways, they had a picture-perfect marriage.

Behind closed doors, the couple struggled with sexual intimacy and impotency issues. In addition, a break in their communication and overall closeness as a couple added stress to the relationship. In an attempt to ease the strain, the wife continued to be patient with the lack of intimacy. However, things came to a head when a female employee at the husband's company stopped by, after work one day, with a garbage bag full of all the gifts given her during the past year. The truth was finally out!

When confronted, the husband admitted to a one-night stand, a lie that tested his wife's understanding and forgiveness. It wasn't a one-night stand, but an ongoing, adulterous relationship. Her heart and trust broken, the wife struggled to believe her husband again. When they sought pastoral counseling, the couple discovered a family pattern of infidelity. Through counseling and with God's help, their marriage was not only restored, but their whole life together became a story of redemption.

They raised four beautiful children together, but their family was challenged once again by sin, when one of the daughters got involved in a sexual relationship before marriage and became pregnant. Heartbroken, the dad went to each of his children and told them about his own adulterous behavior. He repented to each of them for his sin and revealed a generational cycle of sin in the

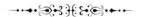

By the power of God's love, you can create a legacy of righteousness, a story of a family redeemed for His purposes.

family. As a family, they prayed together and closed the door to the enemy. Together, they asked God to help them create a new legacy of fidelity and purity in their family. In the power of Jesus' name, they took a stand against this cycle of sin.

Today, as this couple holds their granddaughter, they are filled with the joy of this new life's purity. They moved forward as a family, knowing the goodness of God in life-giving relationships.

The beauty of God's restoration in our relationships is that He brings His redemption—healing to that which is wounded and making whole that which was broken.

God's Redemptive Love

No sin that you have ever committed is so great that God's love can't redeem it. He takes the broken pieces of our lives and fashions them into a mosaic of beautiful glass that His light can shine through. Like the stained-glass windows in a church building, our lives can tell the story of His redemptive love.

If both partners in a marriage are willing to work on the relationship, with God's help, every wound can be healed. Through God's power, every cycle of sin can be broken.

You may not be in control of whether your marriage is restored because it takes two people to work on a marriage. However, you can be assured that God will be with you every step of your journey.

> *For He Himself has said, "I will never leave you*
> *nor forsake you."*
> Hebrews 13:5 (NKJV)

God is with every marriage where the partners call on Him to help. He is also with every family who calls on His name. His story of redemption flows through the generations. Yes, every family and marriage will face sin. The good news is that, on the cross, Jesus already made a way for their victory over the sins—past, present, and future. By the power of God's love, you can create a legacy of righteousness, a story of a family redeemed for His purposes.

Pray in Faith for Your Marriage

Faith-filled prayer inspires hope. As you come into agreement with God's plan for your life and marriage, you are able to walk with positive expectations, anchored in God's faithfulness.

Take some steps right now to pray for your marriage. Use these words as a springboard for prayer. Pray these words aloud:

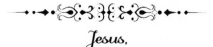

Jesus,

I COME TO YOU ASKING FOR YOUR HELP.

I HAVE OPENED THE DOOR TO THE ENEMY THROUGH MY UNBELIEF.

I CHOOSE TO BELIEVE YOU FOR YOUR BEST IN OUR MARRIAGE.

I HAVE OPENED THE DOOR TO THE ENEMY THROUGH
MY UNFORGIVENESS.

I CHOOSE TO FORGIVE MY SPOUSE FOR _____.

I HAVE OPENED THE DOOR TO THE ENEMY THROUGH MY OWN SIN.

RIGHT NOW, I ASK YOU TO FORGIVE ME FOR _____.

Jesus,

SOAK ME IN YOUR PRESENCE, CLEANSE ME BY YOUR LOVE.

FILL ME WITH FRESH INSIGHT AND POWER
TO CLOSE THE DOOR ON THE ENEMY.

I CLOSE THE DOOR TO HIS LIES IN MY LIFE.

I CLOSE THE DOOR TO UNFORGIVENESS.

I CLOSE THE DOOR TO DESPAIR, RAGE, AND CONTEMPT.

Jesus,

FLOOD ME WITH YOUR LIGHT.

LET THE RAINBOW OF YOUR RESTORATION
PERMEATE OUR MARRIAGE.

LET THE SWEET BALM OF YOUR GRACE
ANOINT THE FRAILTY OF MY FLESH.

LET THE TRUTH OF YOUR PERFECTION
SHOW US THE WAY WE ARE TO WALK.

I trust You. I love You. I believe You.

Expectancy

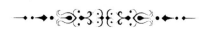

Full of Hope in the Power and Presence of God
Constructive, Positive, Empowering Relationships
Optimistic and Confident in the Word, Will, and Ways of God
Daily Encouragement from God in Prayer
Tangible Love and Hope for the Future
Anticipation of Good

TRAIT 9
Expectancy

On a beautiful fall day when the leaves were brilliant with color, the love of my life took me for a picnic. As we drove down country roads, my husband-to-be looked for the perfect place to take pictures.

The warmth of the sun shone on my face as I posed for the one who loved me so unconditionally. To capture a memory of the two of us sharing this special day, Wayne positioned our old-fashioned film camera on a rock and set a timer.

Just before the shutter released, Wayne looked deep in my eyes and said, "Sue, I want you to know that I believe you have a call on your life. I promise to do everything I can to support you and launch you into all you are called to be." Time seemed to stand still as I comprehended his promise. He was laying down his life for me. Amazed, I looked into his eyes with trust and expectancy. The camera clicked, capturing the intimate moment on film.

When we got the prints back from the developer, we saw the preciousness of that day in a once-in-a-lifetime photo. Even though we had no photographer with us, the composition was perfect. Frozen in time, we were looking into each other's eyes with a rainbow of light covering us.

Every time I see this picture, the rainbow reminds me of Wayne's promise. He had spoken a covenant of love to me in a very private moment and heaven's light was captured in a photograph. The arc of colors framed our faces with radiance of expectancy.

Expectancy in Marriage

At the end of the rainbow of every life-giving marriage is expectancy. It is common to experience expectancy during your engagement or with the anticipation of a newborn child. However, maintaining expectancy in marriage is an important pursuit of a healthy marriage.

But just like acceptance, friendship, safety, honesty, intimacy, passion, endurance, and restoration, if you aren't intentional about maintaining this life-giving trait, expectancy can dwindle, like water down a drain.

OBSTACLES TO EXPECTANCY IN MARRIAGE
1. Boredom: An emotional state resulting from inactivity and a lack of focus. Marriage characterized by routine and predictability. Bored couples have lost their sense of purpose individually and together as a couple.
2. Health Issues: Ranging from common issues caused by lack of sleep and exercise to major illnesses and chronic disease, health problems experienced by one or both partners will impact the marriage. When one or both people don't feel physically healthy, a couple's expectancy and overall sense of well-being can feel diminished.
3. Children: At any age or stage, children complicate the marriage relationship. The extreme joy of introducing a newborn baby to a household also adds immediate complications to making the marriage the cornerstone relationship in a family. As children grow, complex issues ranging from schoolwork and behavior to personal struggles can arise and attack the unity in a marriage and family.

4. Pornography: Pornography distorts a person's perception of sexuality and breaks down the healthy sexual union in marriage. It decreases satisfaction with a partner's appearance and sexual performance. Pornography's addictive quality decreases the ability to be aroused by one's spouse, as increasingly provocative demands must be met to create the same "high."

5. Addiction: Alcohol and drug addictions affect millions of marriages. One of the greatest struggles occurs when an addict maintains that he or she doesn't have a problem. This denial leaves the partner to deal with the brunt of consequences from the addict's behavior.

6. Infidelity: Unfaithfulness in marriage attacks the covenant between a husband and wife. Rationalized in the mind before it is acted upon in the flesh, adulterous relationships occur through deceit. Infidelity, whether it is physical or emotional, destroys the foundation of marriage—one man with one woman for *life*.

7. Abuse: The potential for abuse in the home is great. It is a misuse of power that exploits and takes advantage of trust. When a family is dealing with domestic violence, sexual abuse, or emotional maltreatment, abuse shakes the whole family to its core. Only with the miracle of God's grace can a family recover and heal from abusive situations.

There are many more obstacles to expectancy.
This list is just an example.

Any continued cycle of sin in a person's life has the power to destroy expectancy in marriage. Sin breaks down relationships and builds up barriers. In every marriage relationship, the wounding we experience is from the sin—our own and our spouse's wrongdoings, deceit, selfishness, and prideful natures. We will inevitably hurt and be hurt by our mates. The reality of our universal proclivity to sin and our innate need for repentance and forgiveness is evident in this key Scripture:

For everyone has sinned; we all fall short of God's
glorious standard.
Romans 3:23 (NLT)

The Saving Power of Forgiveness

Throughout this book, we have talked about the power of forgiveness, and I want to bring it up again here, in context not only to your marriage relationship, but also to your relationship with Jesus Christ.

Many people assume they are Christians because they attend church, or, at one point in their lives, said a prayer at an altar, or made a commitment to Jesus at church camp. None of these activities make a person a Christian. To be a Christian, you must have a relationship with Jesus; He must be the Lord of your life. You may have prayed in the past or even pray regularly. The question is: Have you completely and totally surrendered your life to Jesus?

I ask this question at this juncture in the book, in particular, to all of us who live in the United States. It is common, especially in the South, to assume *everyone* is a Christian when, in reality, many people go to church for the same reasons they would

attend a chamber of commerce meeting. Church has become a cultural center where it's easy to make contacts with potential clients and be inspired to live a positive life. But being a Christian is about so much more!

Living as a Christian means that you have totally surrendered to Jesus as your Lord and Savior. You are no longer on the throne of your

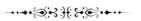

Any continued cycle of sin in a person's life has the power to destroy expectancy in marriage.

life. You serve God daily, and you listen to His Spirit leading and guiding you as you read and meditate on His Word. If you are a Christian, your motives for being part of a church include learning more about Jesus, fellowshipping with other believers, and serving people.

Being a Christian should lead to having a Christ-centered home and marriage. When both spouses live sacrificially, serving each other and wanting the best for one another, they demonstrate the kind of love and forgiveness Christ has for each of us. That's what *should* happen. But our reality isn't always so perfect. Being a Christian is not a foolproof guarantee that you will never divorce. I have counseled many Christians whose marriage has turned around as they surrendered fully to God. I have also counseled Christians who loved God with all of their hearts, minds, and souls, and their marriages still ended because their spouses chose not to honor the marriage covenant. I've said before you cannot control your spouse's behavior; you can only control how you will love and respond to them.

Being a Christian may not guarantee that your marriage will never fail. But as a follower of Christ, you *are* guaranteed to be eternally loved by Him. And when you are in a love relationship with Jesus, you can be certain you will still be fully embraced by His love, even if your marriage ends. You can also be sure that He will give you the strength you need to endure and grow through any challenge in your marriage. He *wants* your marriage to be a strong, beautiful reminder of God's love-filled plan of redemption and unity.

Anchor Your Expectancy on Jesus

If you are a Christian, your first love is Jesus. In a marriage, this doesn't hinder your love life to your spouse. On the contrary, if your hope is anchored in Christ, you are better able to love your husband or your wife.

Expectancy in marriage is not a matter of expecting certain things to happen. Nor is it about having a list of needs and the expectation that your spouse will meet every one of them. If you build your hope on your husband or wife's ability to fulfill all your desires, you will constantly be disappointed. If, on the other hand, you build your hope on the fact that God is good, then your confidence will stand secure, no matter what you face in life and marriage.

With Jesus as your first love, you are able to find your security and confidence in your love relationship with God. Likely, God will lead you to do sacrificial things to show love to your spouse. But your hope is not based on your spouse's actions or reactions. It is anchored on the truth that Jesus loves you, just as He loves your spouse.

The way to ensure your expectation is securely anchored in Jesus is to spend time with Him daily. Spending time with God every day is like a detoxification process. You may come to Him tired, discouraged, and hopeless, but, if you seek God in prayer and read His Word, you will be comforted and strengthened. Choosing to renew your mind daily is a smart choice to cleanse yourself from the toxins of this world.

> *Don't copy the behavior and customs of this world,*
> *but let God transform you into a new person by*
> *changing the way you think. Then you will learn to*
> *know God's will for you, which is good and pleasing*
> *and perfect.*
> Romans 12:2 (NLT)

So many of our expectations for marriage and happiness do not come from God's Word; they come from the media and the world around us. Television programs and movies frequently portray a hero or the heroine choosing to do immoral things to get what he or she wants. And it's so easy to fall in line with the world's way of thinking! For example, romantic comedies lead us to hope that a couple will get together, knowing full well that, in the movies, "getting together" often includes a sexual relationship outside of marriage. While we watch, our minds accept worldly beliefs and behaviors as "normal" and "expected," rather than as sinful and harmful. Bit by bit, our moral standards change, as do our expectations for what romance and marriage should look and feel like. But here's the truth: If you lower the standards of your life and expect to live your life like the people in a movie or soap opera, you are not living God's will for your life.

Let God transform you into a new person every day by changing the way you think. Choose to be intentional about what you think, believe, and do. Learn to think like God thinks by reading His Word daily and spending time in prayer. His will for you is good! You can trust Him to come through for you when everyone else fails. God's will for you is pleasing and perfect.

The Rainbow Promise

God brings out rainbows every time it rains. Only God could think of creating a rainbow of color, caused by the refraction of the sun's light by rain in the sky. After the global flood, God showed Noah a rainbow and told him it symbolized a promise to human kind that He would never again destroy the whole earth with a flood.

The rainbow of promise between a husband and wife is not that each of them will be perfect in their marriage relationship. On the contrary, because every marriage is made up of imperfect people, the imperfection of your marriage will be evident to you and others. Thankfully, our hope is not in our own performance.

If you lower the standards of your life and expect to live your life like the people in a movie or soap opera, you are not living God's will for your life.

Our hope is in the presence of God—that His likeness will refract through our circumstances—good or bad—to make our marriage beautiful.

God's Design for Marriage

Our marriage vows, made in the presence of God and witnesses, celebrate the miracle of oneness. God brings a husband and wife together in "holy matrimony," so that the beauty and power of His presence can be multiplied in their lives together. And, *yes*, He has a purpose for your marriage! God desires to build His kingdom and advance His message through the evidence of His presence in your lives. Together as a couple, you are messengers.

Your message as a couple can carry the purity of His redemption through the frailty of human relationship. Even though we have talked about the pain within marriage in this book, nothing can compare with the blessing and wonder of oneness in marriage. The ecstasy and beauty of being one with another human being brings the power of heaven to earth.

God has designed your marriage to be an encouragement to other couples. Your marriage can grow up like a strong tree planted in the soil of God's Word. Each year of your marriage is like a ring on a tree. Some years, you may experience drought. Those are the years that your roots will reach even deeper into the soil to be fed by the underground stream of God's refreshment. And through every storm you weather together, your marriage grows because your life and strength comes from Him.

God uses your spouse, your disagreements, and

---•·→•·⟨⊛⟩·3 ⟩⟨ ⟨·⟨⊛⟩·•→•·---

God uses your spouse, your disagreements, and your faults to help you become more like Him.

---•·→•·⟨⊛⟩·3 ⟩⟨ ⟨·⟨⊛⟩·•→•·---

your faults to help you become more like Him. Having freed you from the selfish, self-centered nature of this world, His desire is that your life will point others toward the grace of His redemptive plan. We know God intends for us to share His message of salvation and reconciliation.

> *Therefore, if anyone is in Christ, the new creation has come: The old has gone, the new is here! All this is from God, who reconciled us to himself through Christ and gave us the ministry of reconciliation: that God was reconciling the world to himself in Christ, not counting people's sins against them. **And he has committed to us the message of reconciliation.***
> 2 Corinthians 5:17-19 (NIV, emphasis added)

In his book, *Sacred Marriage: What if God Designed Marriage to Make Us Holy More Than to Make Us Happy* (Zondervan), Gary Thomas explains how God's message of reconciliation can be seen through marriage.

> *Everything I am to say and do in my life is to be supportive of this gospel ministry of reconciliation, and that commitment begins by displaying reconciliation in my personal relationships, especially in my marriage.*
>
> *If my marriage contradicts my message, I have sabotaged the goal of my life: to be pleasing to Christ and to faithfully fulfill the ministry of reconciliation, proclaiming to the world the good news that we can be reconciled to God through Jesus Christ.*

Every day, as you trust His promises and choose to love and forgive your spouse, you set an example for your children and others in your life. Your commitment allows others to see that a Christ-centered marriage is a *life-giving marriage* full of expectancy for a beautiful future together.

Loving God and Maker of all the earth,
IT WAS YOUR PLAN AND DESIGN TO CREATE MARRIAGE.
YOU PURPOSED IN YOUR HEART TO MAKE MY SPOUSE AND ME.
THROUGH OUR UNION, YOU BRING LIFE.
FREE US FROM EVERY DESTRUCTIVE HABIT.
Give us fresh courage to pursue You and Your dream.
WE CHOOSE TO FULLY SURRENDER TO YOUR WORD,
YOUR WILL, AND YOUR WAY.

OUR EXPECTANCY AND HOPE IS ANCHORED IN YOU.
WE CHOOSE TO LIVE IN FORGIVENESS EVERY DAY,
KNOWING THAT YOU ARE THE LIFE-GIVER.
WE DESIRE FOR YOUR LIFE TO FLOW THROUGH US,
TO EACH OTHER, AND OTHERS.
OUR TRUST AND HOPE IS ANCHORED IN YOU.

YOU ARE THE FULFILLMENT OF EVERY DREAM;
YOUR LOVE COVERS A MULTITUDE OF SINS.
LET US BE REMINDED EVERY DAY TO CARRY
YOUR LIGHT AND LOVE TO A LOST AND DYING WORLD.
You are our joy and delight.

WE THANK YOU THAT OUR RELATIONSHIP WITH YOU
NEVER ENDS.
You are the Eternal Life-Giver.
WE PLACE OUR MARRIAGE IN YOUR HANDS.
IN YOUR NAME WE PRAY,
AMEN.

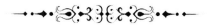

Conclusion

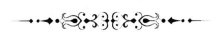

What a joy and a privilege to walk with you through the course of this book! As Wayne and I have taken a risk to share the intimate details of our marriage with you, we hope and pray you have grown in your knowledge of what it means to have a life-giving marriage.

As a couple, you have the opportunity to allow the Spirit of God to make your marriage a masterpiece. We pray that your marriage will be a sign that points to the goodness of God in how He has worked miracles in your marriage.

God desires for marriage to draw us into a closer relationship with Him—unity with Him enables us to have a *life-giving marriage*. Before we close the book, I'd like to review the nine traits that will help strengthen your relationship with God and your spouse. As you attempt to incorporate these traits into your marriage, remember that God doesn't expect for you, on your own, to become the husband or wife your spouse needs. It is His grace that transforms you into a person capable of the love and respect necessary for a strong, healthy marriage. When you review these nine traits, please do so with the faith that in the areas where your marriage presently falls short, God is able to transform you and your relationship by His power.

Acceptance

With the joy-filled realization that you and your spouse each have God-given gifts, you are able to affirm the uniqueness of who you are individually and as a couple. You are both being perfected by God's grace. Acceptance means you welcome the differences your spouse brings to your marriage. You respect his or her rights and ability to make choices. Neither of you controls or manipulates in the marriage. Instead, you choose to trust in the transformative power of God to bring life-giving changes in each of your lives.

Friendship

Your spouse really can be your best friend—someone to whom you are emotionally bonded. As friends, you find joy in being together. You choose to share the intimate details of your life with each other, to listen and comfort in the face of pain and sorrows. Because a friend loves at all times, you share the joy of daily life and learn to let go of irritations and petty offenses. You choose to enjoy your differences and build a unity of being one. You protect the powerful bond of your marriage covenant. You nurture your relationship by choosing to spend time together daily.

Safety

In a healthy life-giving marriage, you are open and unafraid to be yourself. You are emotionally free to be vulnerable with your spouse. Your home and relationship is a place of refuge. You shelter each other from storms of life. There is a security in your relationship with God and your spouse. You are truly at home in the arms of the one you love.

Honesty

Being honest is a choice and promise that strengthens marriage. Your sincerity and candor are spoken with love. You are open to receive truth-filled words and choose to speak with respect, not contempt. You are transparent, allowing God's light to shine in and through you. Your life is characterized by honorable integrity. You are trustworthy and dependable. You have a real marriage and deal with real problems, yet your heart is pure as you share with Spirit-led sensitivity.

Intimacy

The affectionate friendship of your connection with your spouse fosters an emotional, spiritual, and physical intimacy. You find pleasure in each other's company. You are passionate for the purposes and plans of God. Your shared love and closeness are found first in your relationship with God and then with each other.

Passion

As the strong emotion of love draws you together, you revel in the joyous truth that God made sex between a husband and wife to be good—to be holy. With a commitment to undying passion, you keep the flame burning in your desire to be intimate emotionally, spiritually, and physically. You keep yourself wholly committed only to your spouse. You find pleasure, satisfaction, and fulfillment in your passion for one another.

Endurance

Your endurance grows as you are willing to walk in consistency. Your emotional, physical, and spiritual connections to your spouse are anchored in God's love. Because of God's love, you are able be patient and persistent. Your character is marked with perseverance and restraint. You determine in your heart to be loyal. As you look back over your marriage, you are amazed at your God-given capacity to overcome difficult circumstances. With tenacity, you hold on to God's purposes for your life, including your unyielding commitment to your marriage.

Restoration

Through every struggle, harsh word, or mistake, God offers the restoration of His redeeming love. Trust in Him to find healing from your own brokenness and to help your spouse experience God's healing. Your passion for your spouse will go through cycles, but God's love continues to rejuvenate your tenderness and love.

Your relationship has been and can be again repaired through the power of the cross. Rebuild intimacy by claiming your call and purpose as a couple.

Expectancy

Because of God's goodness, you are full of hope. Your relationship is flooded with the power and presence of God. Your marriage is constructive, positive, and empowering. You are optimistic and confident in the Word, will, and ways of God. You find daily encouragement from God through prayer. Your visible love and hope for the future is contagious.

Nothing Is Impossible with God!

With God, all things are possible! Trust in that truth, as you place your expectancy in God and anchor your hope in His love. He won't fail you. He is the Life-Giver. It is from Him that you gain strength every day. As you stay connected to God and His purpose, I know you will experience life in your relationship and home.

And the best news? His life and love last for *eternity*.

We would love to connect with you! If you are in the United States, you can text the word MARRIAGES to 33444 and immediately receive information about our upcoming marriage conferences.

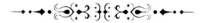

Life-Giving God,
ALL THAT I AM PRAISES YOUR NAME.
WITH MY WHOLE HEART, I PLEDGE MY LOVE TO YOU.
I WILL NEVER FORGET THE GOOD THINGS YOU HAVE DONE FOR ME.
YOU BRING HEALING TO MY MIND, HEART, SOUL, AND BODY.
YOU FORGIVE ALL MY SINS AND HEAL ALL MY DISEASES.
YOU REDEEM MY LIFE FROM DEATH.

YOU CROWN ME WITH LOVE AND TENDER MERCY.
YOU FILL MY LIFE AND MY MARRIAGE WITH GOOD THINGS.
YOU RENEW MY YOUTH AND MY ZEAL FOR LIFE.
YOU ARE COMPASSIONATE AND MERCIFUL.
YOU ARE SLOW TO BECOME ANGRY.

Your love is unfailing.
YOUR TENDER STRENGTH MAKES ME STRONG.
YOUR FAITHFULNESS TO ME HELPS ME
TO BE FAITHFUL TO MY SPOUSE.
YOU HAVE MADE THE HEAVENS AND THE EARTH.
NOTHING IS IMPOSSIBLE WITH YOU!

I GIVE YOU OUR MARRIAGE,
TRUSTING YOU AS THE LIFE-GIVER
TO BREATHE FRESH LIFE INTO OUR MARRIAGE.
I TRUST YOU TO BREATHE LIFE INTO ME.
I BELIEVE YOU, GOD, TO MAKE OUR MARRIAGE
A MASTERPIECE OF YOUR DESIGN.
UNIQUE. SIGNIFICANT.

Together, pray this prayer of dedication.

MAKE OUR MARRIAGE
A CARRIER OF YOUR PRESENCE AND YOUR POWER IN OUR HOME.
MAKE OUR MARRIAGE
A SIGN THAT POINTS TO YOU.

AS YOU HAVE HEALED AND RESTORED US,
WE TRUST YOU TO CONTINUE THE GOOD WORK YOU HAVE BEGUN.
AS WE LIVE OUT THESE TRAITS OF A LIFE-GIVING MARRIAGE,
MAKE OUR MARRIAGE A WELL OF REFRESHMENT AND LIFE
TO OTHERS.

LOVING GOD,
YOU HAVE GIVEN EACH OF US INDIVIDUAL GIFTS.
WE COMMIT TO BE DREAM-RELEASERS IN EACH OTHER'S LIVES.
YOU HAVE ALSO GIVEN US A CALLING AS A COUPLE
TO UNIQUELY SHOWCASE YOUR LOVE TO OTHERS.
WE EMBRACE OUR GOD-GIVEN CALLING
TO ENCOURAGE OTHERS
THROUGH THE LIFE THAT WE LIVE TOGETHER.

WE BELIEVE YOU, THAT YOU WILL USE US POWERFULLY!
WE BELIEVE YOU, THAT OUR MARRIAGE WILL BE
STRONG AND VIBRANT!
WE BELIEVE YOU TO MARK US WITH A MESSAGE OF YOUR LOVE.

OUR HOPE IS IN YOU.
WE LOVE YOU!
IN JESUS' NAME WE PRAY,
Amen.

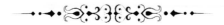

Resources

Marriage and Parenting Help

Family Life Today (familylifetoday.com)
Focus on the Family (focusonthefamily.com)
Marriage Helper Seminar for Troubled Marriages (joebeam.com)
Reignite Your Marriage (smalley.cc)

Help for Lives in Crisis

The National Domestic Violence Hotline
(thehotline.org or 800-799-7233)

Resources and counseling for sexual abuse
(insight.org/resources/topics/sexual-abuse/)

Acknowledgments

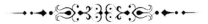

My heart is filled with deep gratitude.

To my Love, Jesus, how You love me. Your love is the most powerful force in my life. Your truth sets me free, to be all that I am called to be. Your grace empowers me daily. Your faithfulness endures when things are hard. You know my every need. I want to share Your love and presence with everyone I meet. I have been so transformed by You that I want everyone to know You intimately. The words of this book are my sack lunch offering to You. Just like You used the loaves and fish that the little boy gave to You, I pray that You would take this book, bless it, and multiply it to be shared with the ones who need the message in these pages.

To my husband, Wayne, you are the love of my life. Patient, gentle, and kind, you walk in the fruit of the Spirit every day. Your character and integrity provoke me to be a better person. Our common love and loyalty for Jesus have guided our life and home. Your encouragement strengthens me. Your love surrounds me. We are His workmanship, and He designed us to be side-by-side, sharing the good news of His message together. What a joy!

To my parents: Donna, you marked me for ministry while I was still in your womb. You claimed Jeremiah 1:5 in my life: "I knew you before I formed you in your mother's womb. Before you were born, I set you apart and appointed you as my prophet to the nations." Allen, you called out my gifts of leadership, ministry, and writing. Before you died, you challenged me to write every day.

To our married children: Rachel and Dustin, Angela and Bryan, what a wonderful delight to see you happily married and well on your purposeful paths as married couples. To Hannah Elizabeth and Sarah Faith, we are praying diligently for Jesus Christ to be the first love of your life and for husbands who will love Jesus even more than you do! To Alexandre Joel and Ezequiel

Paul, we are praying that you become men of God with character, wisdom, and integrity to be husbands who treat your wives with tenderness, love, and strength.

To my team: Erin Casey, your skills as a writer and editor have strengthened me to develop this message. To Lynn and Benita, thank you for your friendship and passion to get this message out. To Marty and Lindsey, thanks for investing your gifts in me and helping this message to be multiplied into the hearts of many.

To the body of Christ: Glenn Burris, Tammy Dunahoo, and The Foursquare Church, your commitment to strong life-giving marriages within the global church inspires us to share this message globally. To David Coffey, Kim Pitner, and the MidSouth District, thank you for the open invitation to plant Life Bridge Church in the North Dallas area. To Pastor Jeff Lamont and Pastor Brad Mathias, thank you for your friendship and partnership in spreading the good news of Jesus Christ's love and power through Life Bridges. To Pastor Eric and Susan Hullett, thank you for welcoming us to the big state of Texas. To Life Bridge Church, though you are just being planted, we pray for life-giving marriages and healthy relationships to be a mark of who we are as a church. To the many pastors, leaders, and intercessors around the world who have taught me and prayed for me, thank you.

About the Author

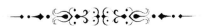

Sue Detweiler is a wife, mother of six, author, and pastor with more than twenty-five years of experience in marriage, ministry, and education. She is also a popular speaker who shares her heart and wisdom internationally on issues related to marriage, family, women, prayer, leadership, and ministry.

Sue's first book, *9 Traits of a Life-Giving Mom*, hit No. 1 on Amazon's hot new releases for Christian women's issues. Her newest book, *9 Traits of a Life-Giving Marriage*, grew out of her and her husband's heart to help couples grow closer to God and to each other. In their pastoral ministry to marriages, they have seen how sharing their own struggles helps to create a safe context for couples to be transparent and honest with their own issues. Wayne and Sue have also seen God's transformative power heal and restore marriages through the marriage conferences and workshops they have led.

For more books and resources or to schedule a speaking engagement, visit SueDetweiler.com or email info@suedetweiler.com.

Background

Sue responded to God's call on her life out of heartfelt obedience to what the Bible commands. Sue and her husband Wayne began in ministry as youth pastors. They moved to Nashville in 1986 and planted and pastored Harmony Christian Fellowship for nine years. During this time, Sue received her Master of Divinity from Vanderbilt University.

Sue and Wayne became a part of The Foursquare Church through their roles as associate pastors at New Song Christian Fellowship. Sue had the privilege of overseeing Life School of Ministry, a Bible training program which helps students develop their ministry gifts. She was also the principal at New Song

Christian Academy, a homeschool program for kindergarten through eighth grade. Sue also partnered with her husband, Wayne, in marriage ministry.

Connect with Sue:

Twitter: @SueDetweiler
Facebook: Facebook.com/SueDetweiler7
Linkedin: Linkedin.com/in/suedetweiler
Pinterest: Pinterest.com/SueDetweiler
Online: SueDetweiler.com and LifeBridgeChurch4.com

Help Us Build a Bridge!

Sue and her husband, Wayne, have recently relocated north of Dallas to Frisco, Texas, to plant Life Bridge Church. Commissioned as church planters with The Foursquare Church, they are also church planters with ARC Churches. Presently, they are looking for 100 innovative leaders to help launch Life Bridge Church, with January 31, 2016 targeted as "Launch Day." To learn more, go to LifeBridgeChurch4.com.

the *Marriage* BRIDGE

CPSIA information can be obtained
at www.ICGtesting.com
Printed in the USA
FSOW02n2337090615
7772FS

9 781943 613007